MW01688455

Best wishes,

Owen Hughes

We Love Tasmania

Photographs and design by Owen Hughes
Text by Martin Gilmour and Owen Hughes

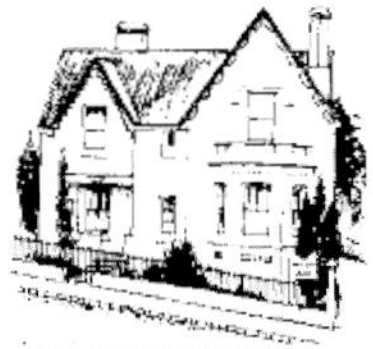

'GREEN GABLES'

PUBLISHED & DISTRIBUTED BY OWEN HUGHES

17 Elizabeth Street, Launceston, Tasmania 7250, Australia. Telephone: (03) 6331 1481

http://www.computermania.com.au/owenhughes/

First Published 2006

Typeset by Computer Support Tasmania, Lilydale, Tasmania 7268, Australia

Colour separation, printing & binding: Dai Nippon Printing Co. Printed in Singapore.

National Library of Australia ISBN number: 0-9590145-7-8

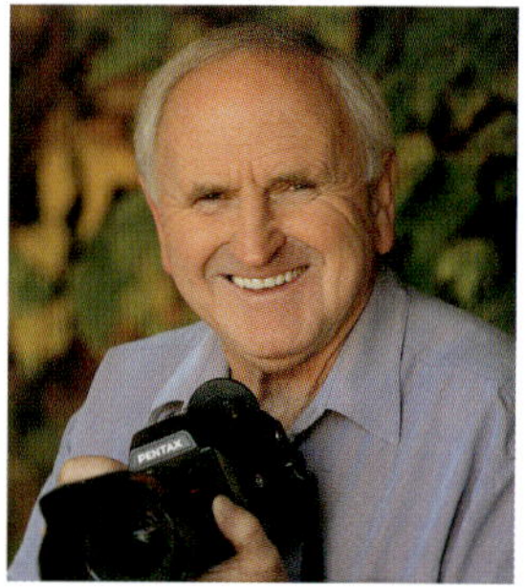

Owen Hughes was born at St. Marys, Tasmania in 1940 and raised on a small East Coast farm where he developed a great love of nature and people. Owen developed a new and innovative style of photography which won him many awards throughout the years including Master of Photography and Fellow of the Australian Institute of Professional Photography. Other awards have included Australian Landscape, Australian Portrait and Australian Wedding Photographer of the Year.

CONTENTS

Front cover: Dawn on the Tamar River.
Back cover: Wineglass Bay, Freycinet National Park

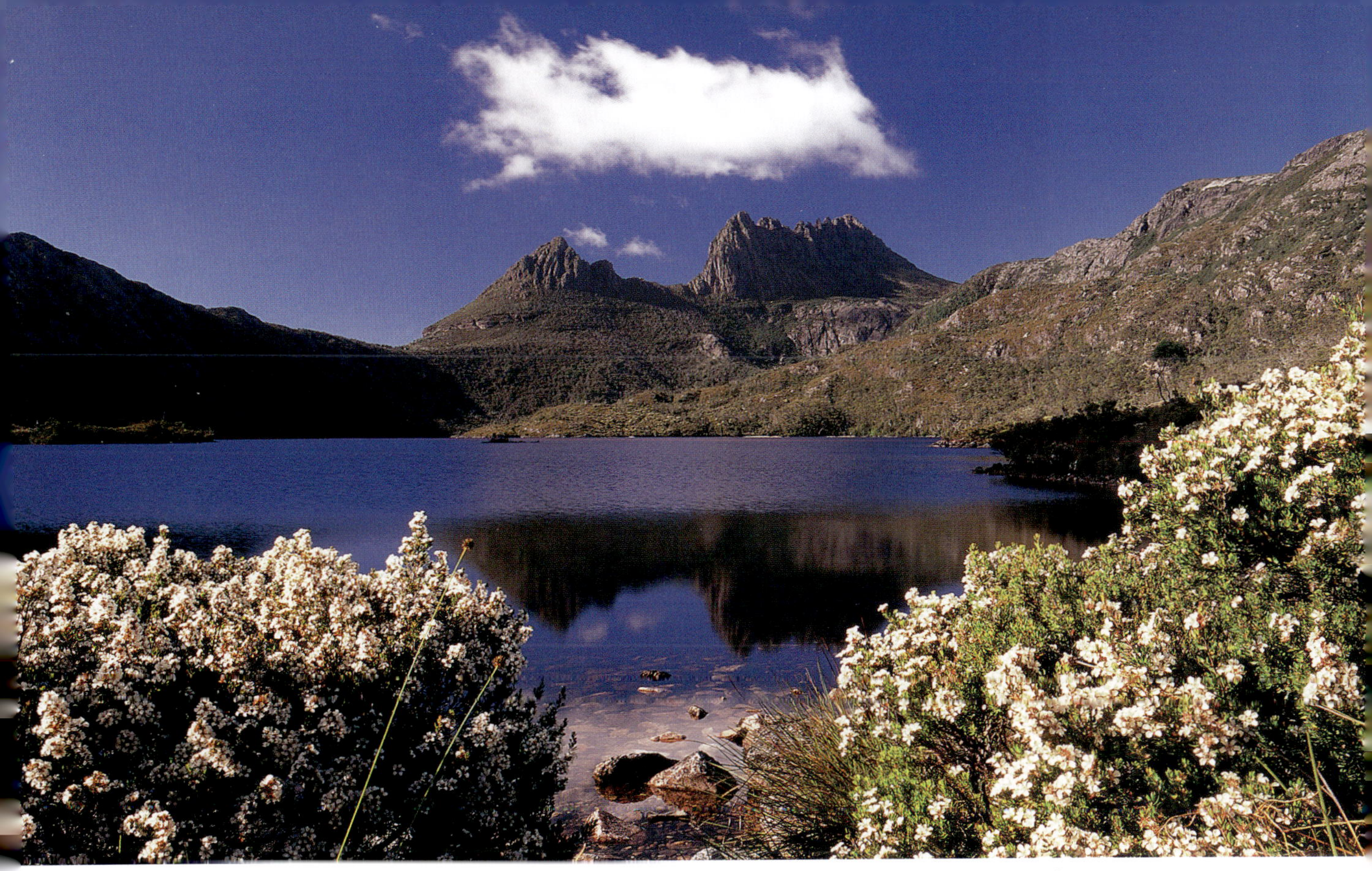

Wild flowers bloom in Summer. Dove Lake, Cradle Mountain.

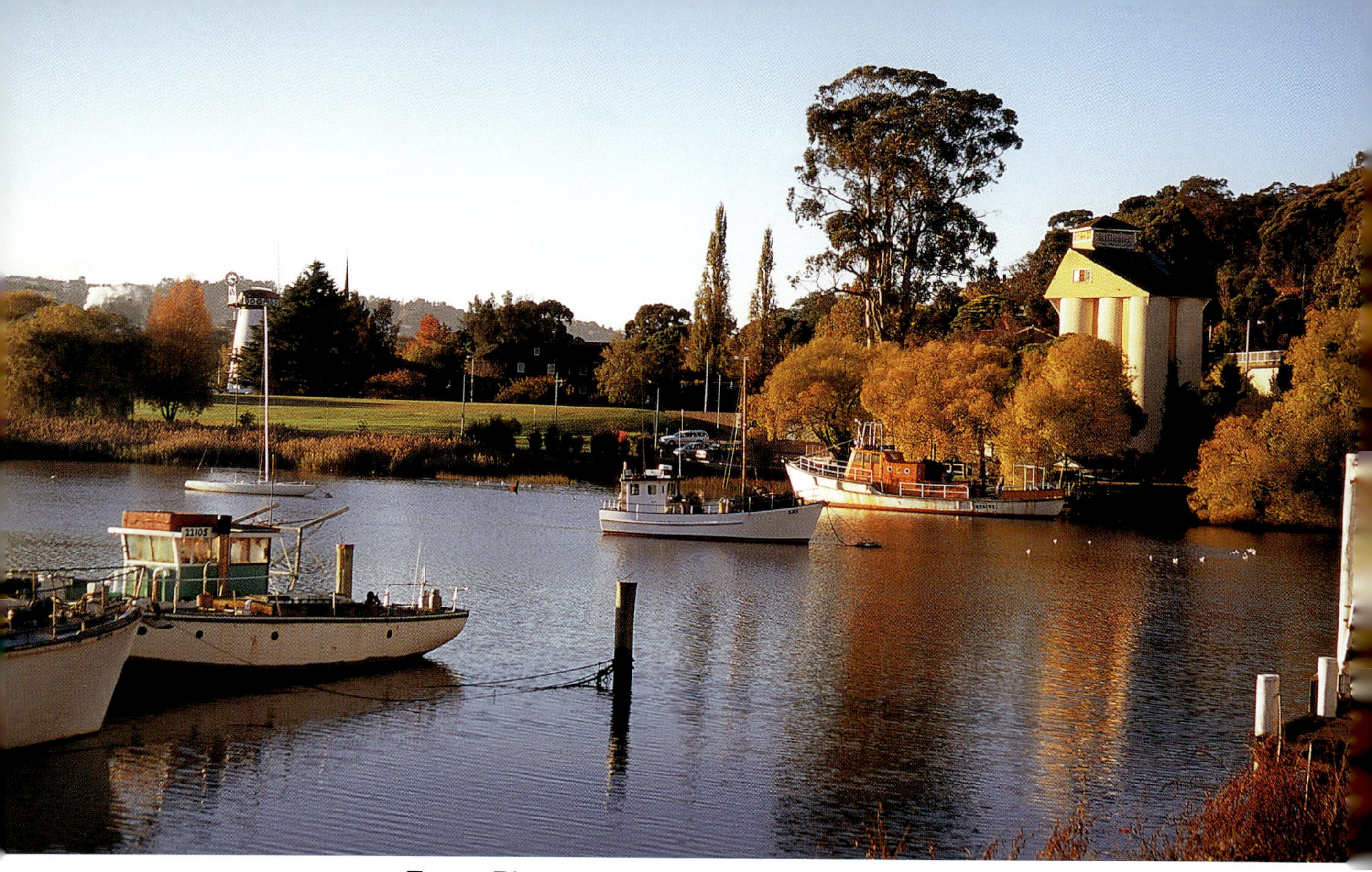

Tamar River and Ritchie's Mill, Launceston

INTRODUCTION

A wild stretch of water 240km wide called Bass Strait separates Tasmania from mainland Australia - it also protects a way of life jealously guarded by many people.

Tasmania is more than an island with ragged peaks, wild rivers, chalk white beaches and rolling pasture land.

It represents a rare quality of life. Smog is unheard of, children grow up with values and opportunities are limited only by an individual's imagination.

As quality of life becomes an ever-pressing goal for many people, so the diverse attraction offered by Tasmania becomes more attractive.

There is a wonderland of natural beauty with more than 96 national parks and reserves occupying over 2,500,000 hectares.

The rich convict background, where thousands of men and women were transported, many for trivial crimes, is intrinsically woven into everyday life.

The stark beauty of early colonisation pitted against the harsh and unyielding elements is preserved for all to remember.

Port Arthur and the Isle of the Dead, Port Macquarie and the ring of mountains which forced escaped convicts to cannibalism in their quest for freedom - it all remains.

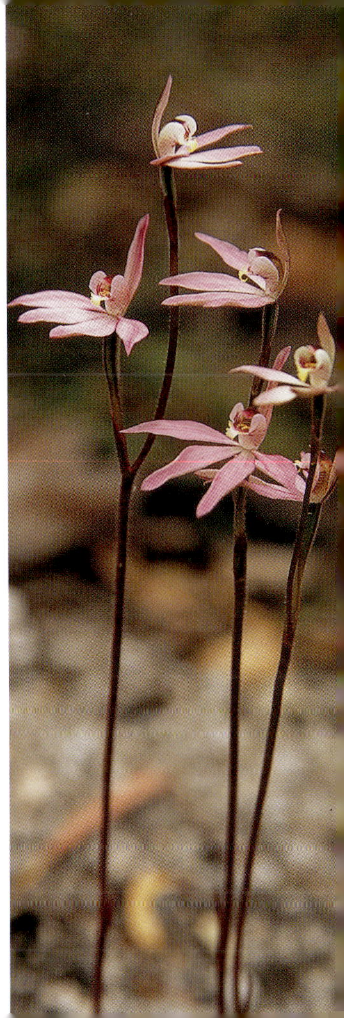

Alpine Caladenia

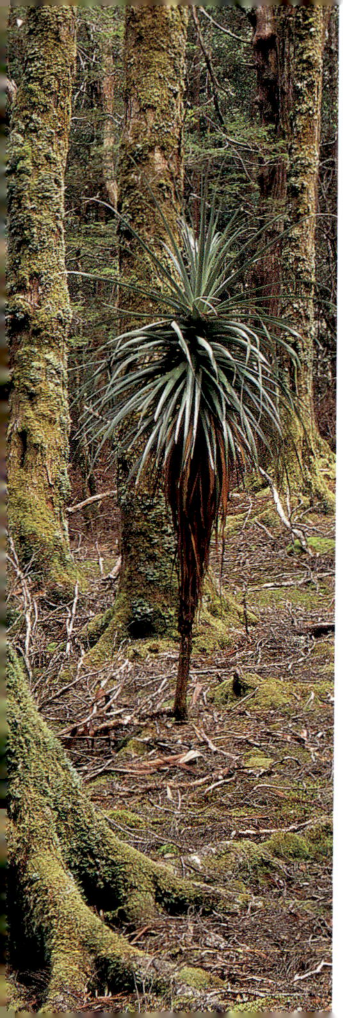

Tasmania is legitimately called the most English of all Australian states.

The orchards, hawthorn hedges and hop-fields; the wild lake country; the early freestone architecture and the roadside villages dotted with elms, oaks and poplars.

But more prevalent is the stunning array of natural beauty.

The likes of Cradle Mountain with its untamed and often deadly beauty; the highland tarns of which many are still unnamed and the rugged South-West wilderness with rivers powerful enough to carve gorges through mountains and turn the tide of governments.

It is no surprise that Tasmania has become a paradise for tourists.

Within an hour by car from any part of the island the terrain can change from deserted beaches, to pasture land, rain forests and eventually wilderness.

Just as close is a first class hotel or the sophistication of casinos and fine dining.

Tasmania is not perfect, bit it is blessed with a special touch of old world magic.

Pandani in myrtle forest

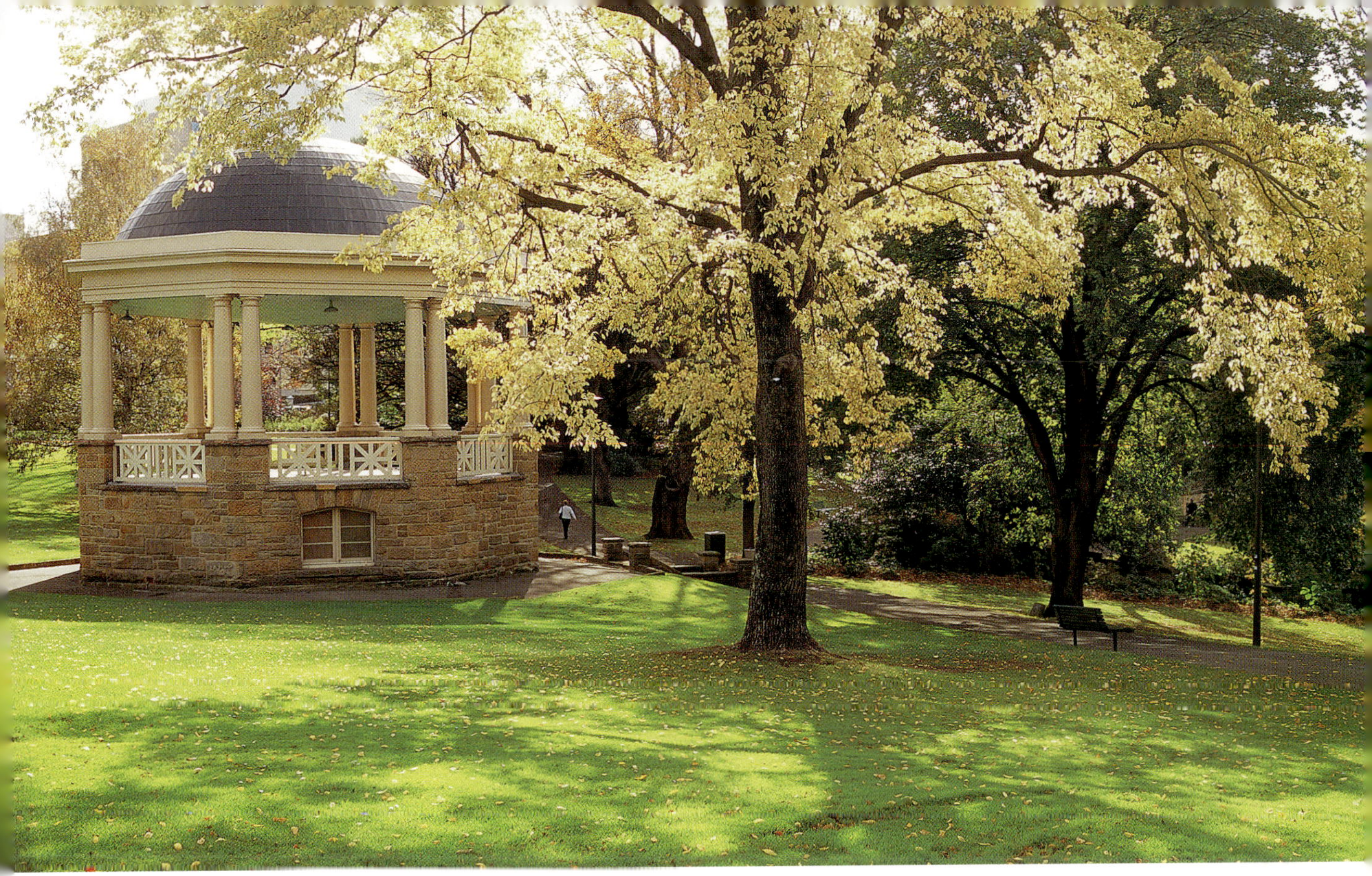

St. David's Park, Hobart

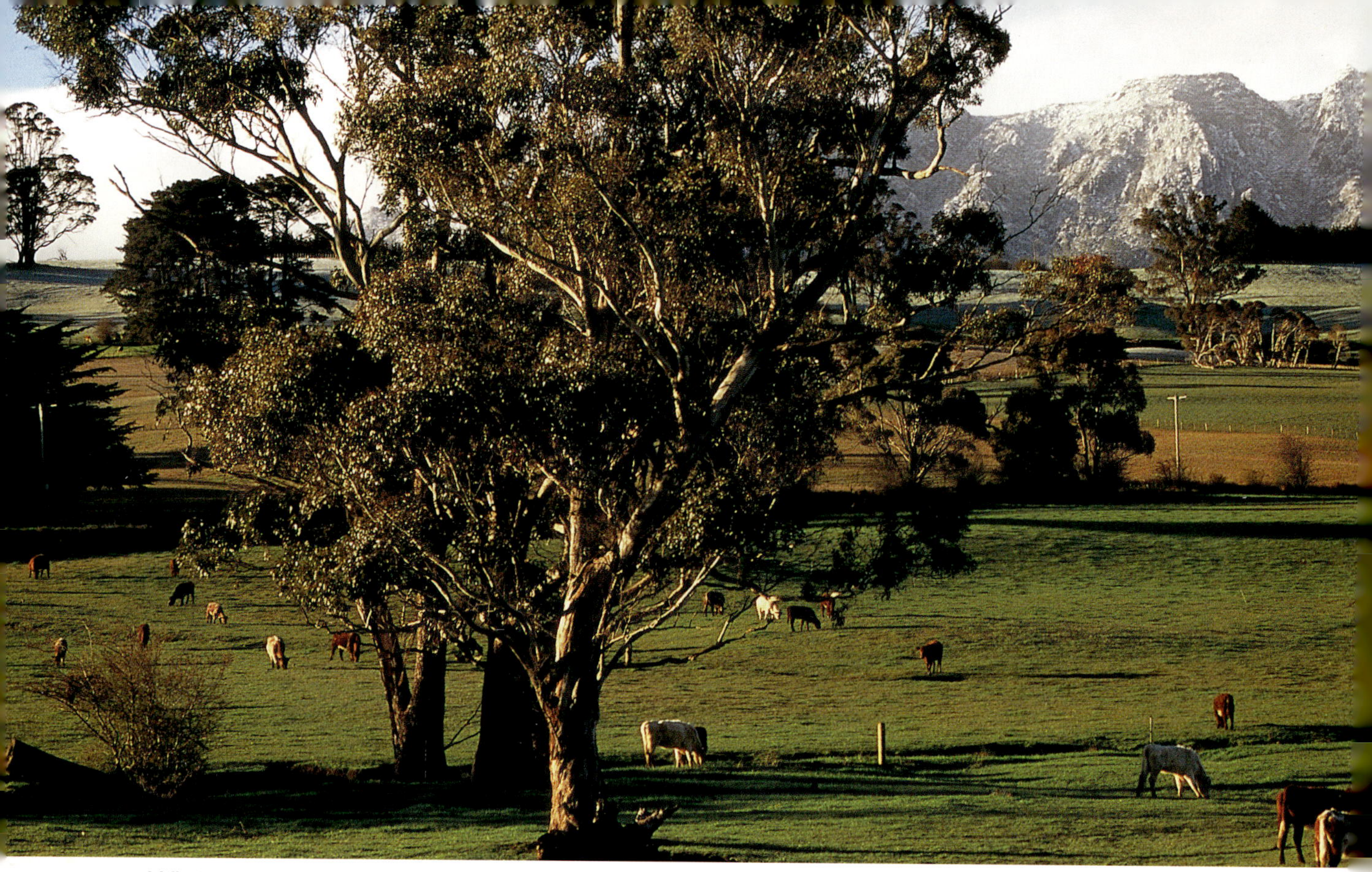

Winter snow on Mt. Roland near the mural town of Sheffield, North-West Tasmania.

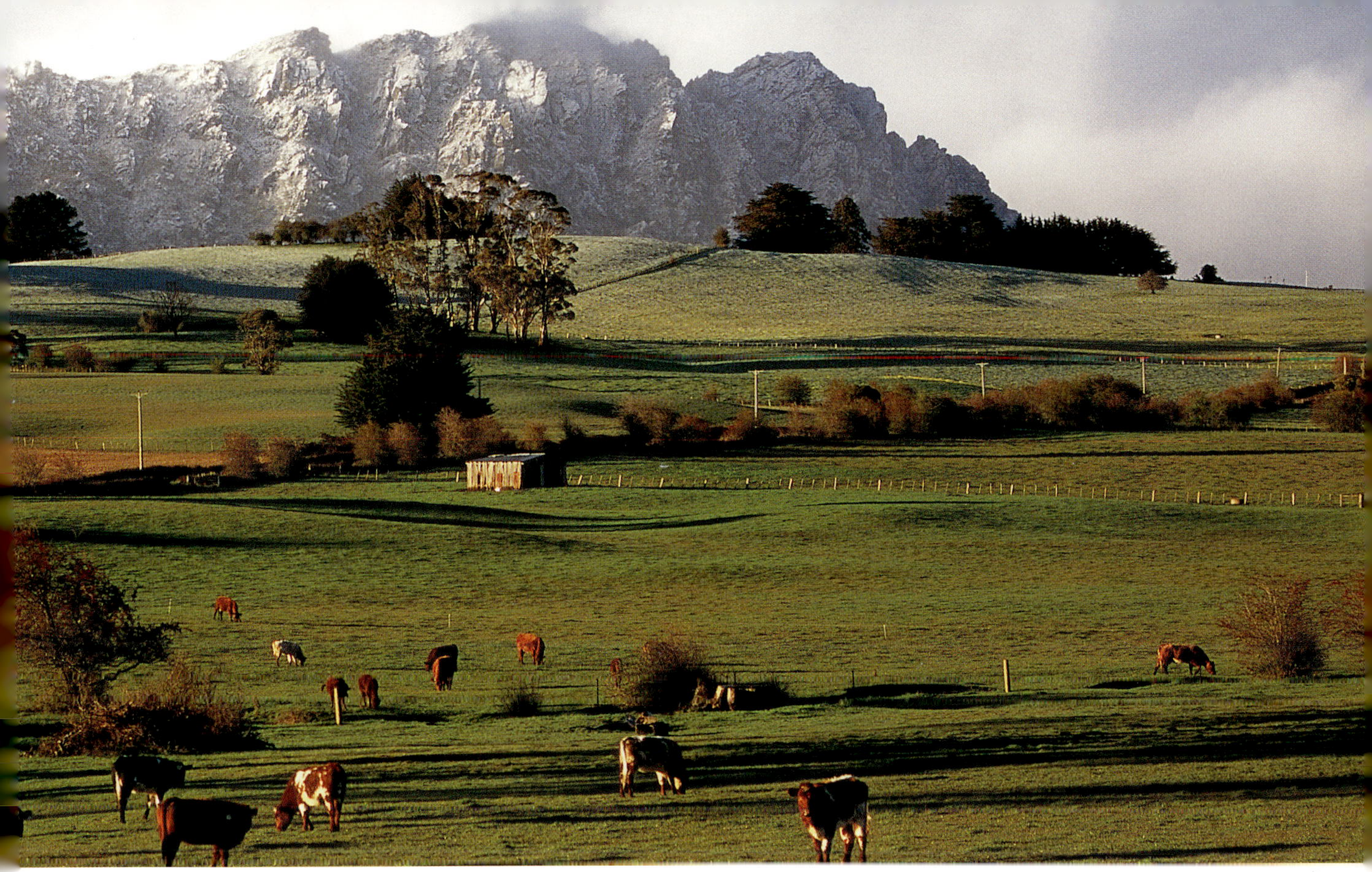

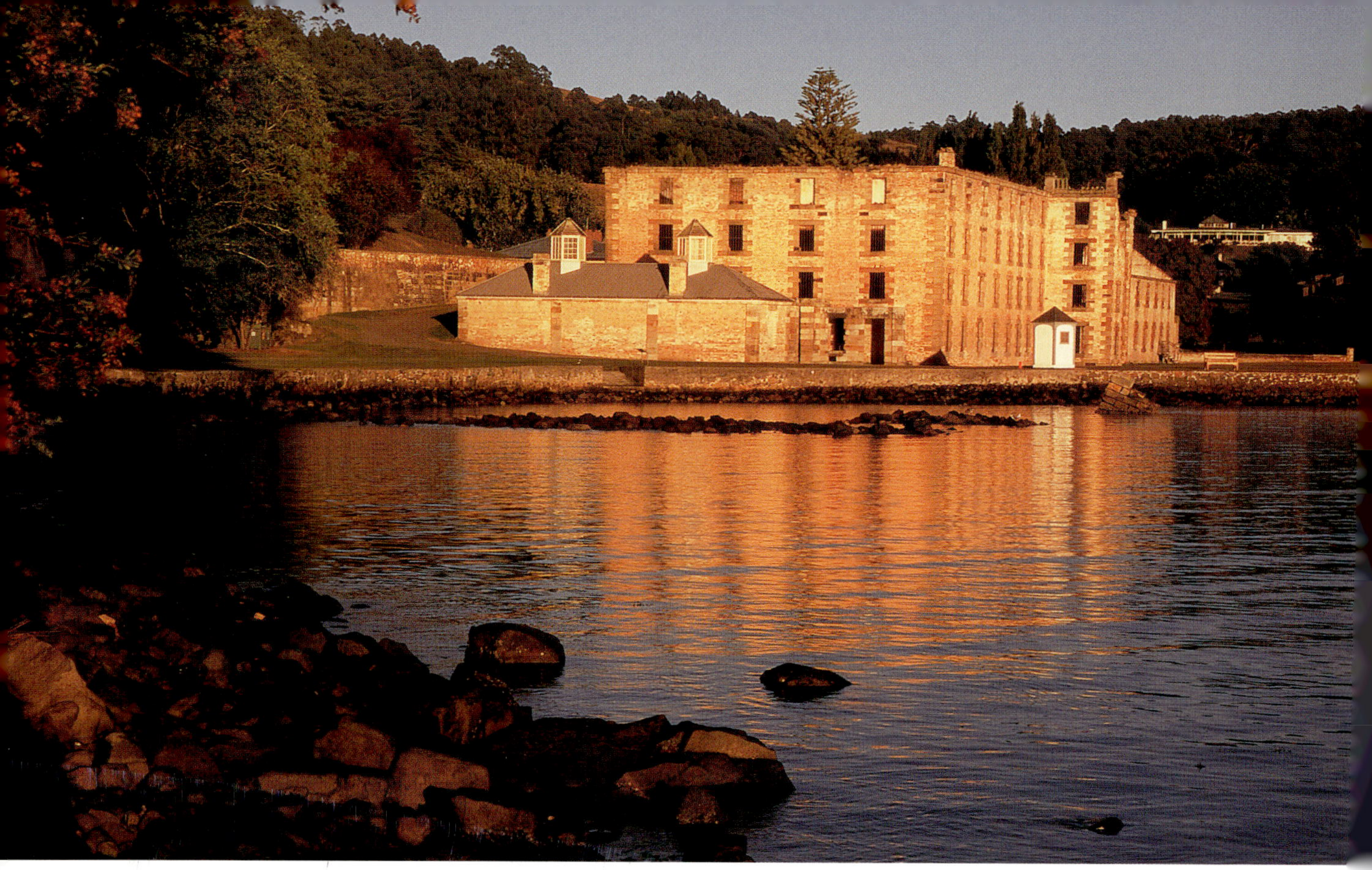

The Penitentiary, Port Arthur ruins.

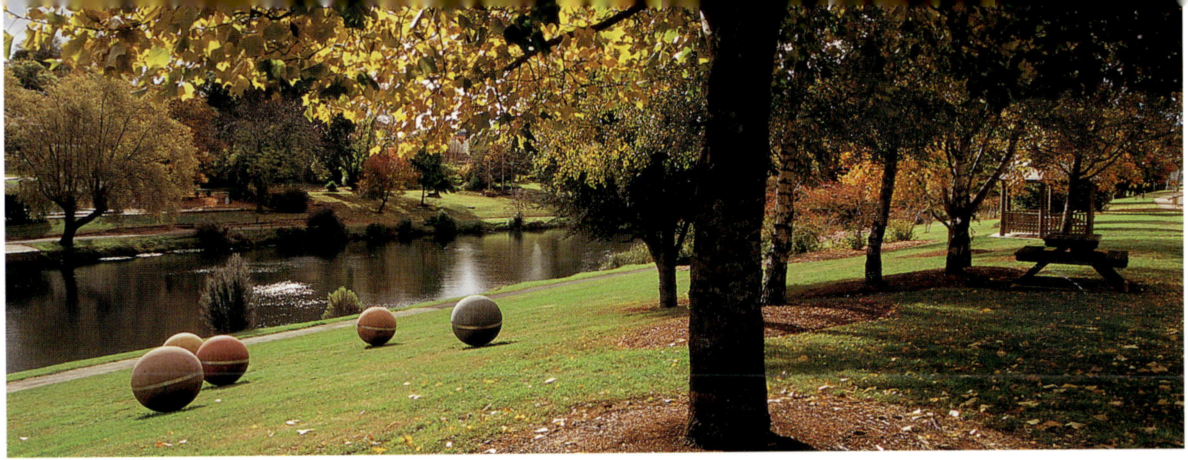

The gardens along the banks of the Meander River at Deloraine.

Historic homestead, Brickendon, at Longford.

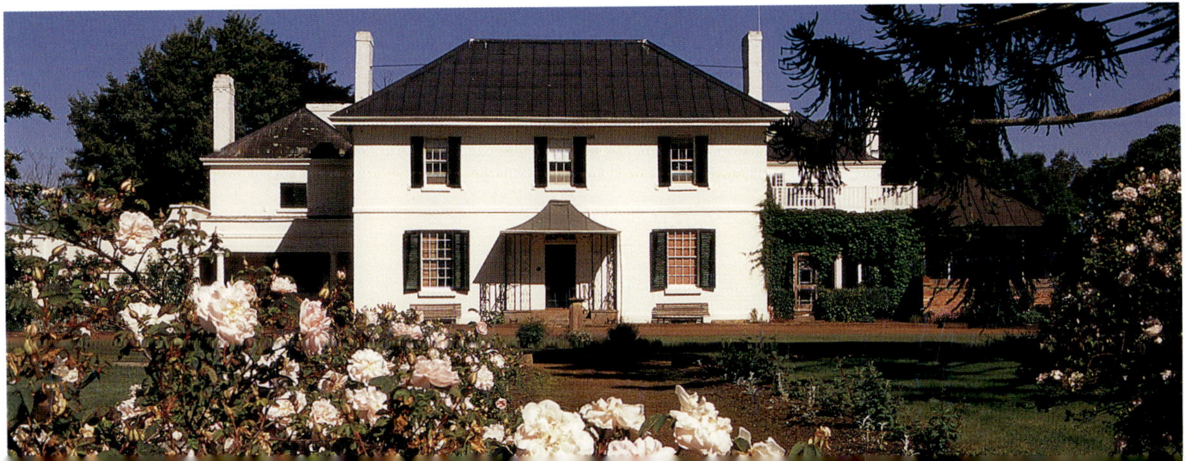

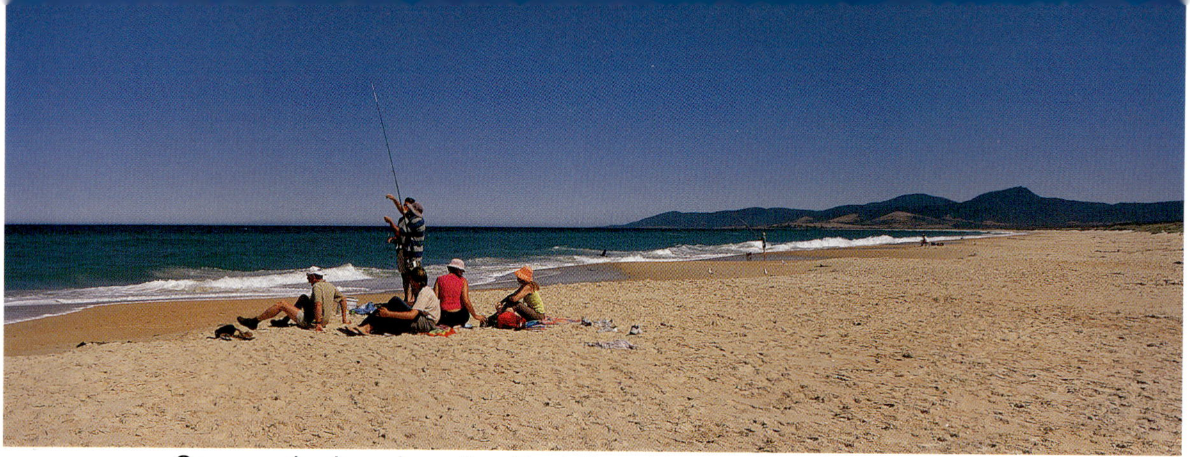

Scamander beach on the East Coast is popular with surf fishers.

The National Rose Garden at historic Woolmers Estate (1816) near Longford is planted with over 2000 roses.

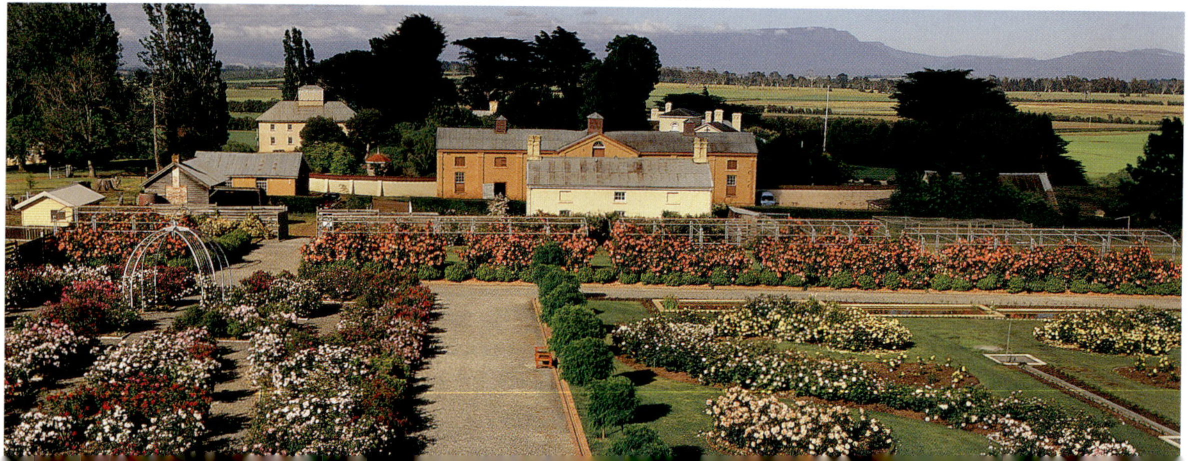

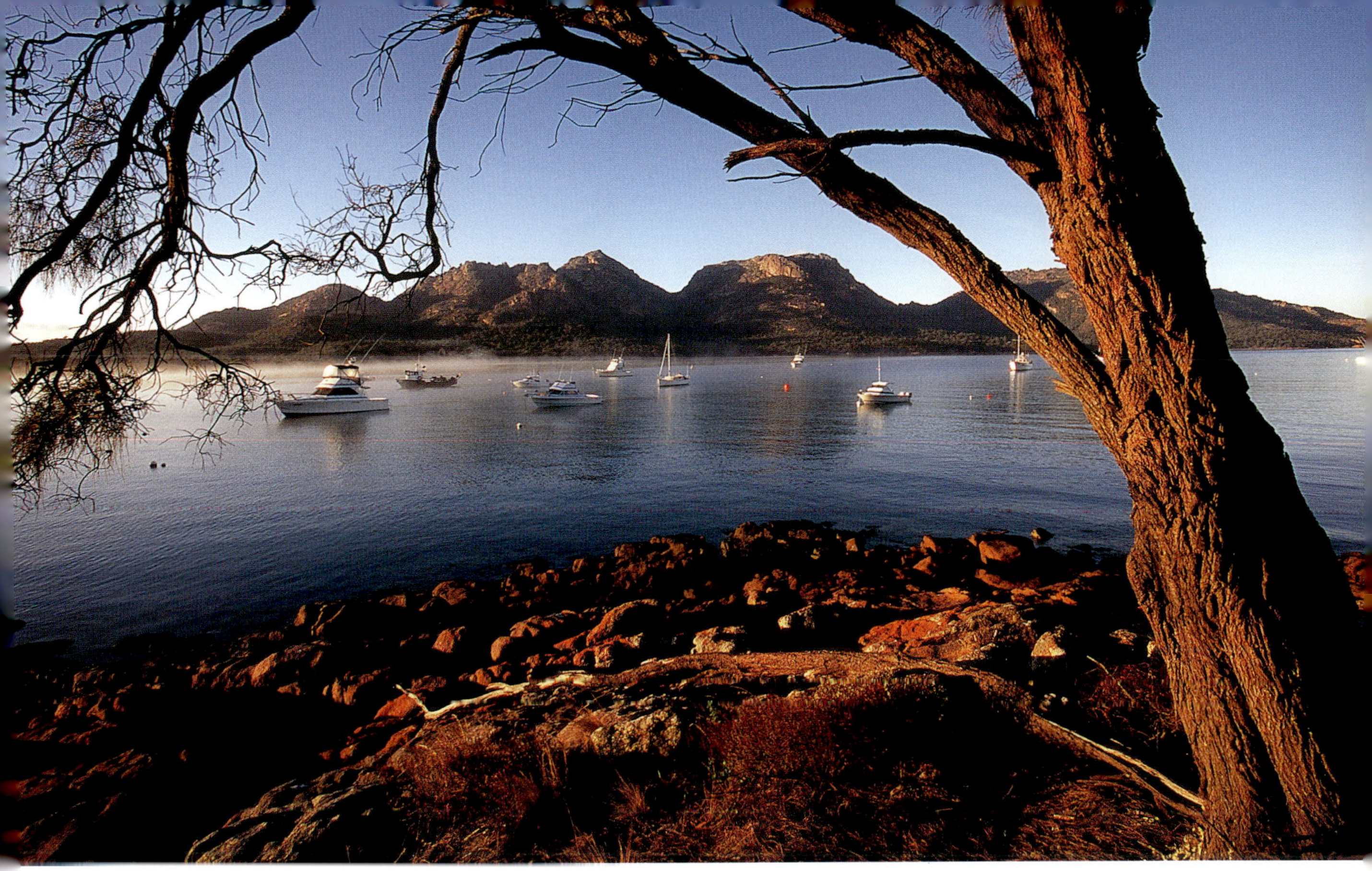

A hint of early morning mist rises at Coles Bay, Freycinet National Park.

THE SOUTH

Nestled beneath the grandeur of Mt. Wellington is Tasmania's capital city Hobart, one of the most attractive capitals in Australia.

It is a city based upon its life link, the Derwent River.

Australia's blue water yachting classic the Sydney to Hobart race ends in the Derwent River and nearly half the city's employees commute across the river to work.

Few people realise Hobart is Australia's second oldest city, being founded in 1804 by John Bowen.

Historically, Hobart and southern Tasmania is a gold mine.

Salamanca Place on the waterfront boasts Georgian warehouses dating back to the whaling days of the 1830s which are occupied today by restaurants, art galleries, craft shops and taverns. Every Saturday morning the area springs to life with the famous Salamanca Market.

A short distance from Salamanca Place is Battery Point, the original quarters for the seamen of Hobart Town.

The area is unspoilt with quaint cottages flanking narrow lanes and village greens.

Hobart has many buildings classified by the National Trust including Australia's oldest theatre, the Theatre Royal, built in 1837.

There are many fascinating attractions in and around Hobart.

Most visitors to southern Tasmania rarely leave without seeing Port Arthur and the settlement of Richmond.

Port Arthur is about 100km. from Hobart on the Tasman Peninsular.

This area of Tasmania is famous for the penal settlement between 1830 and 1877.

Just off-shore from Port Arthur is the Isle of the Dead where more than 2000 convicts, free men and soldiers were buried during the life of the settlement.

Richmond arguably has the greatest concentration of historic buildings in a small area and is only 30 minutes drive from Hobart.

About an hour's drive from Hobart is Lake Pedder and Lake Gordon which are equally popular for their trout fishing and breath-taking scenery.

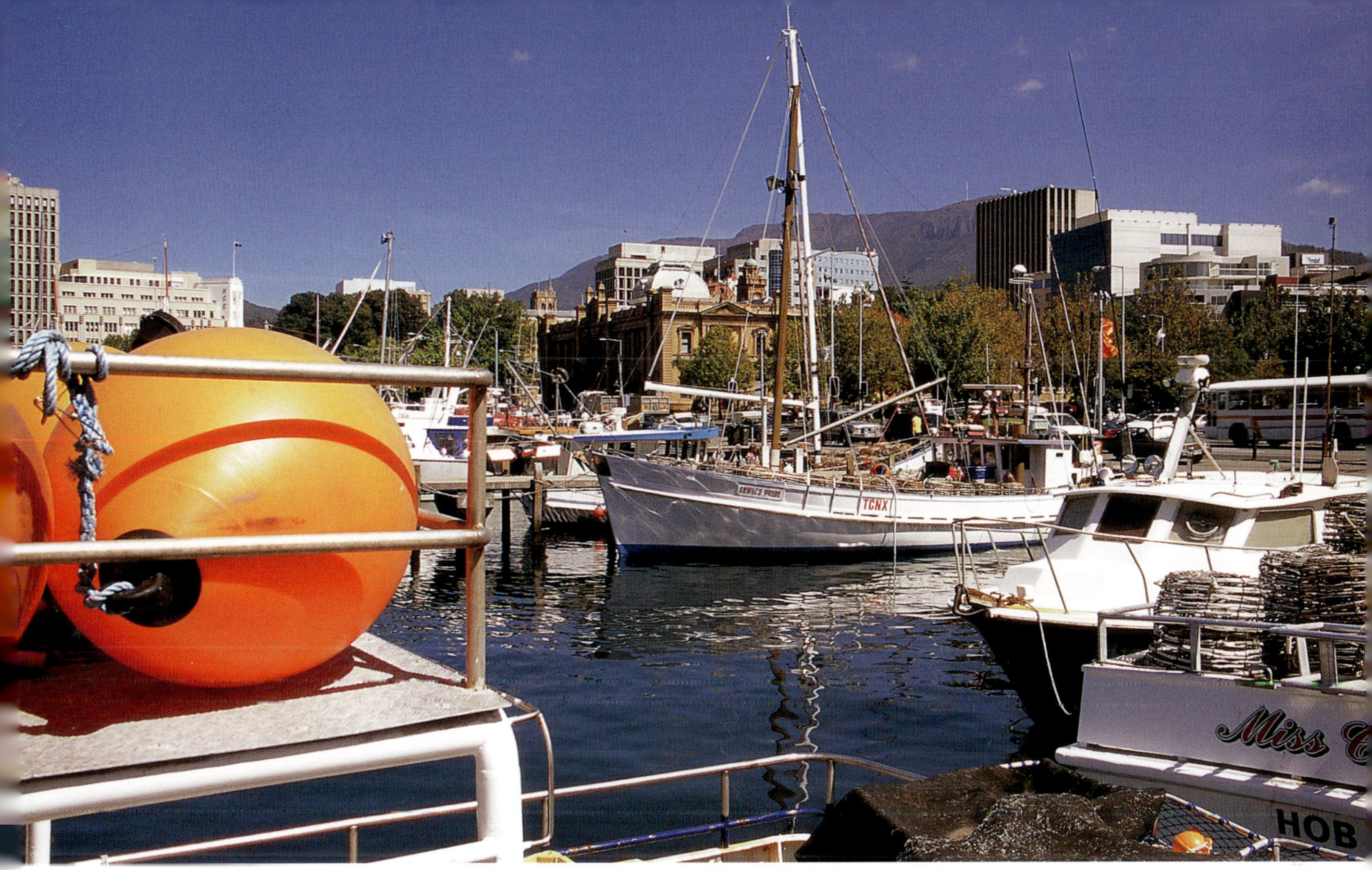

Fishing boats at rest, Victoria Dock, Hobart.

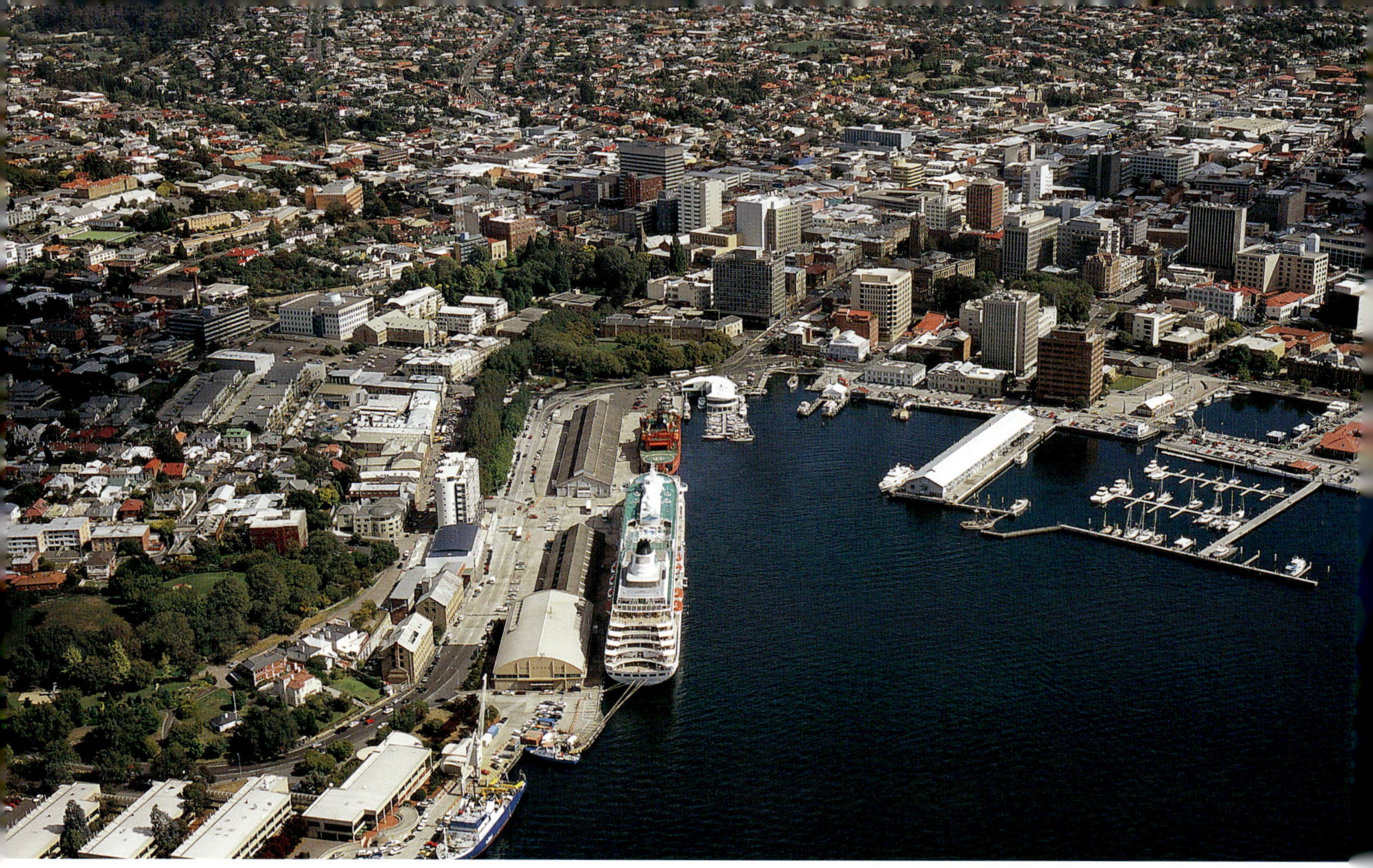

Aerial view of the Hobart waterfront.

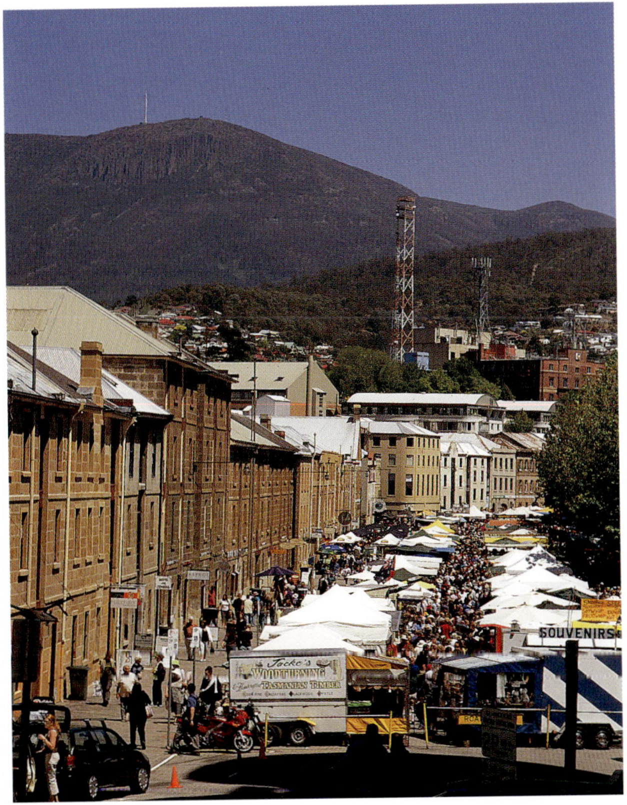

Salamanca Market and Mount Wellington.

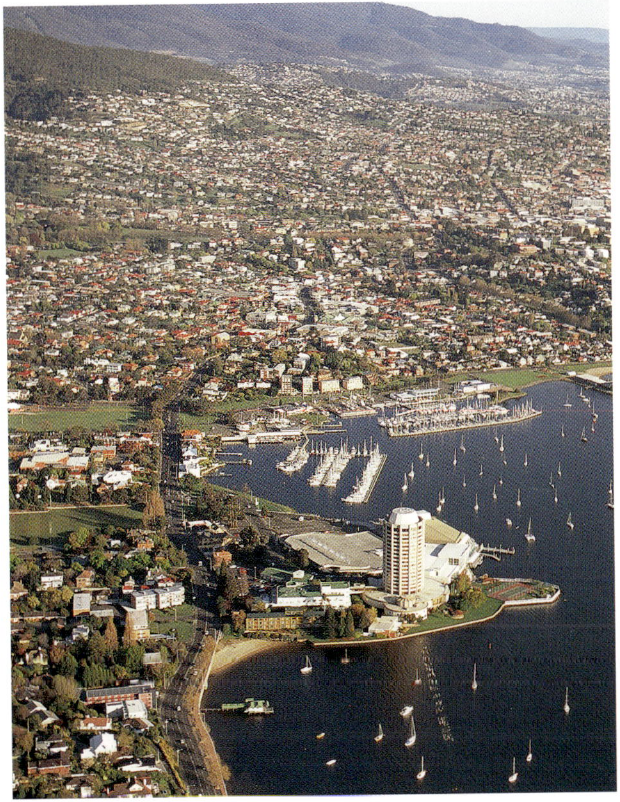

Wrest Point Casino at Sandy Bay.

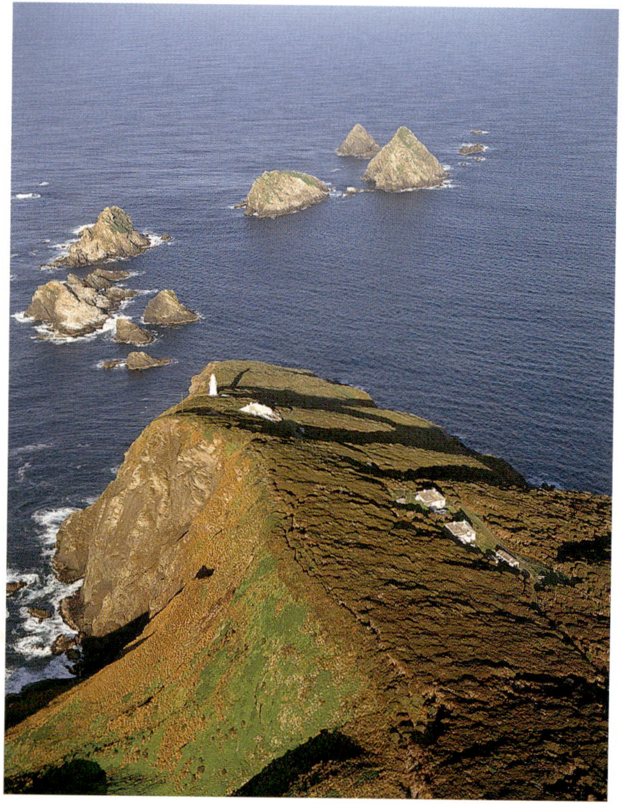

Maatsuyker Island, Australia's southern most lighthouse

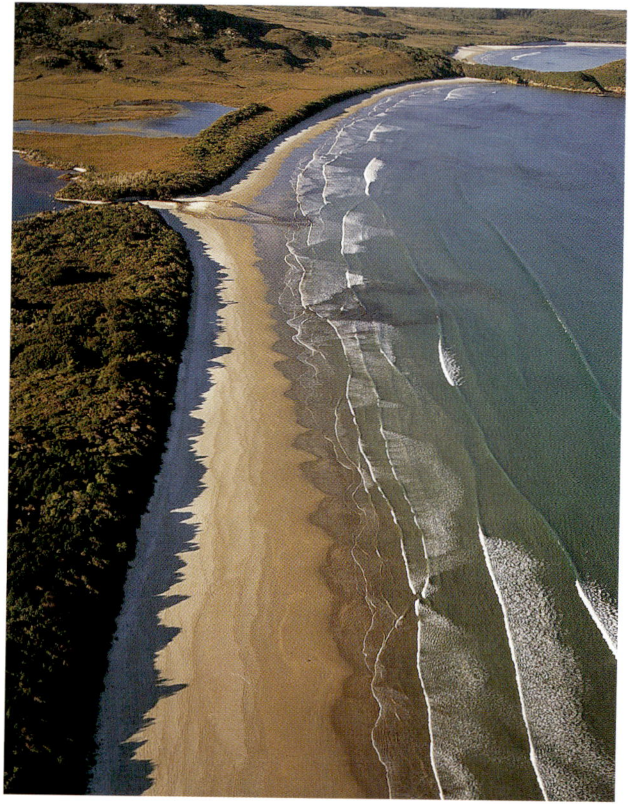

Cox Bight, Southwest National Park.

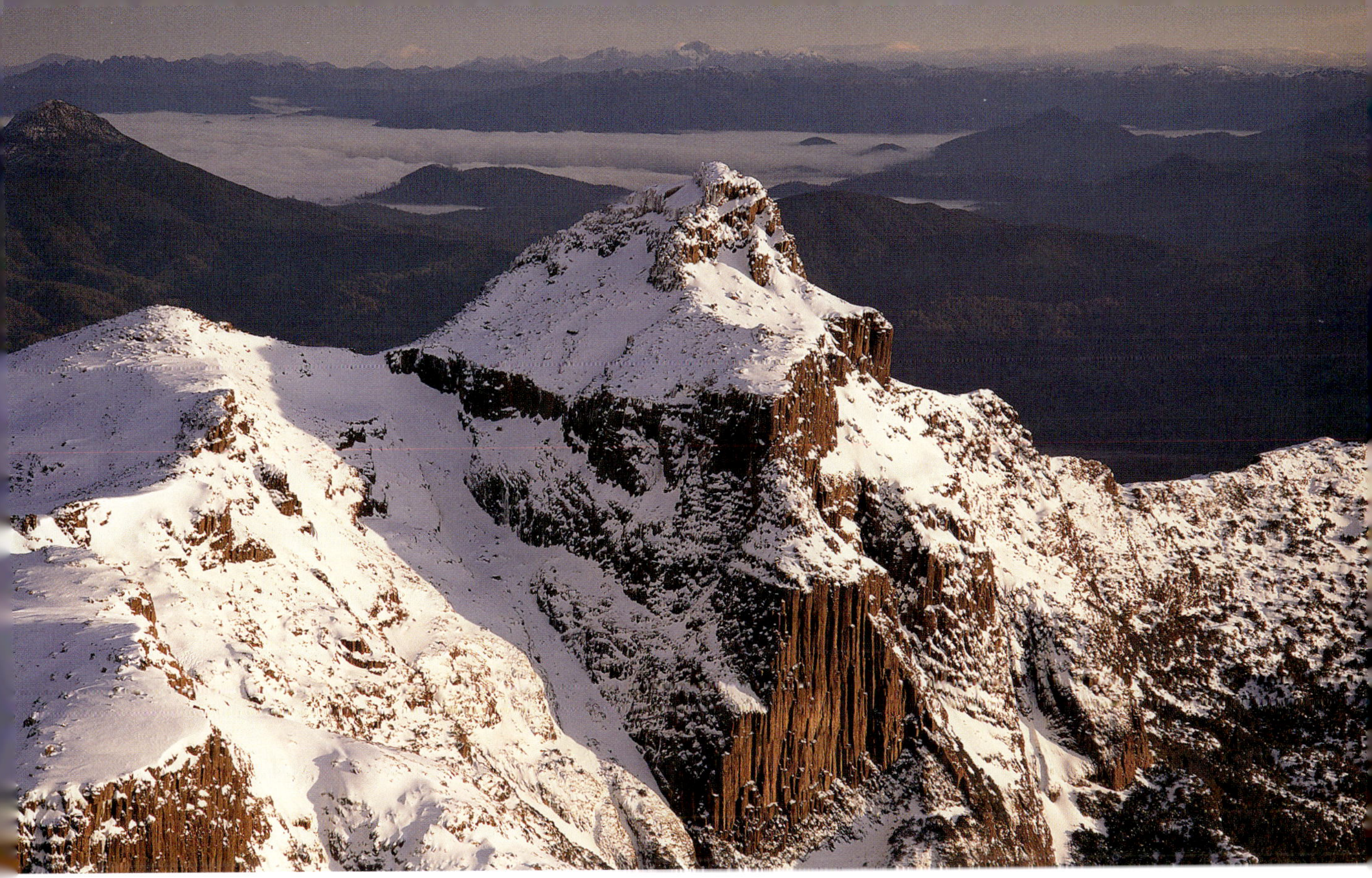

Mt. Anne, Southwest National Park.

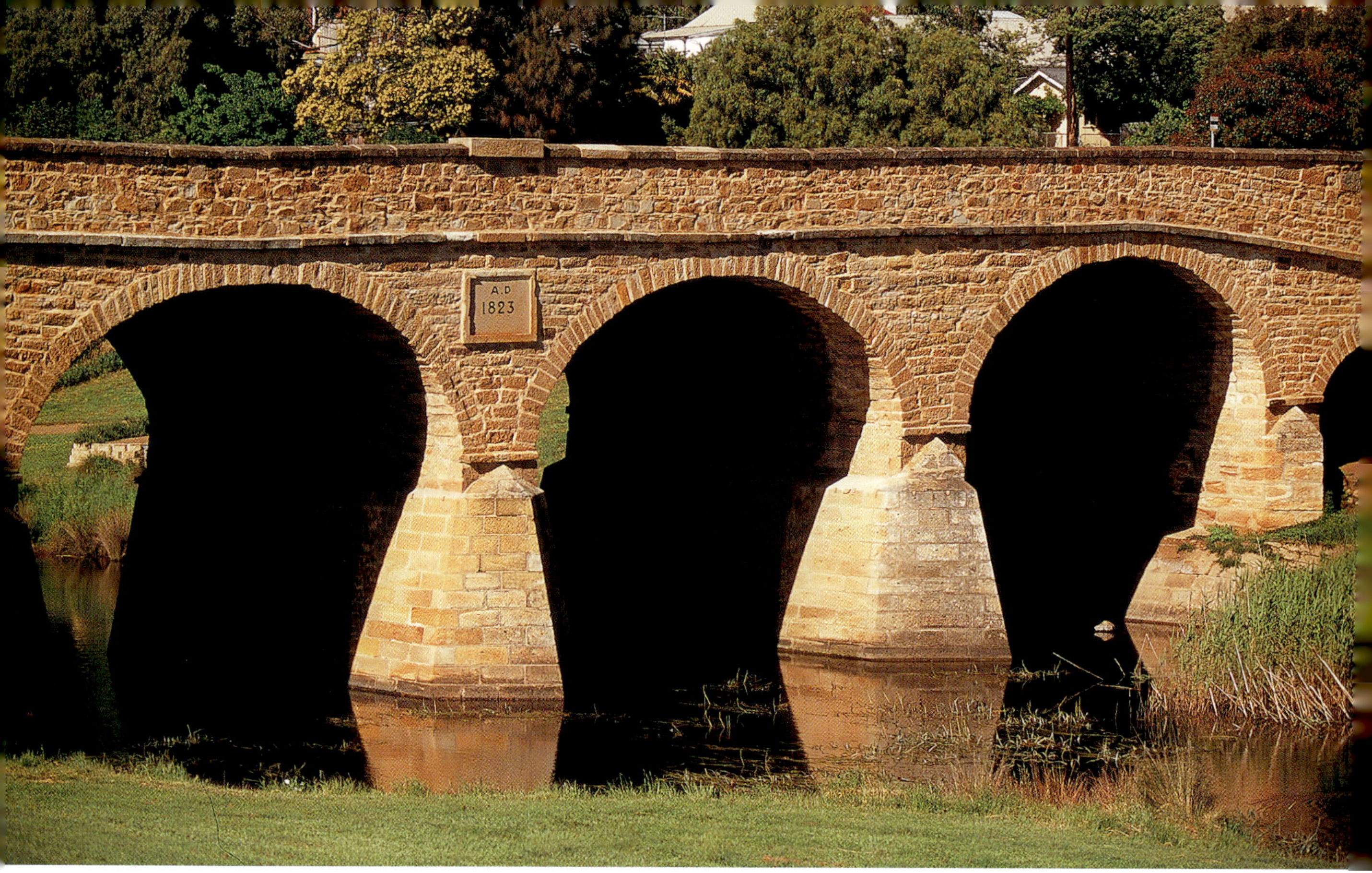

Richmond Bridge (1823) is Australia's oldest.

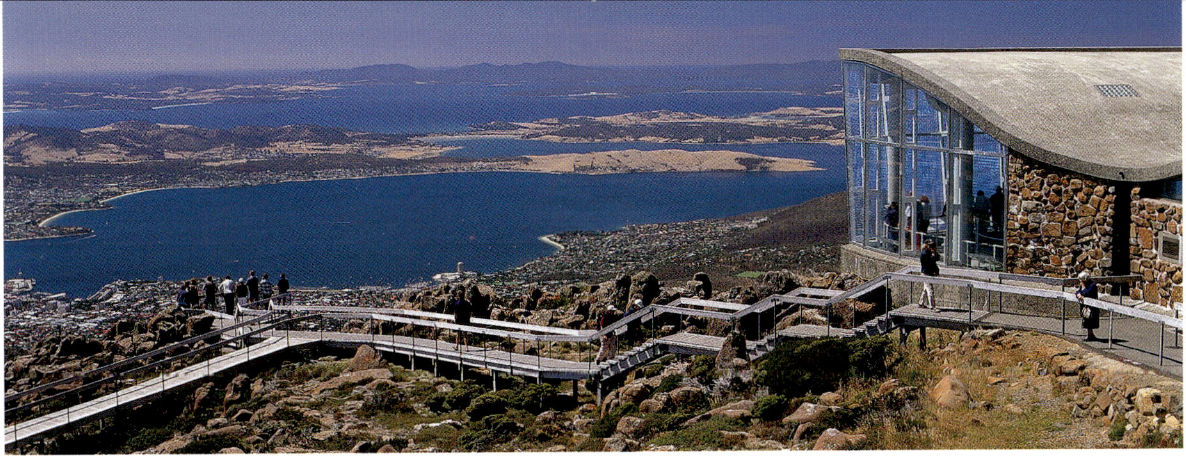

The view of Hobart and the Derwent River from Mt. Wellington.

Port Esperance at Dover with Anderson's Peak in the background.

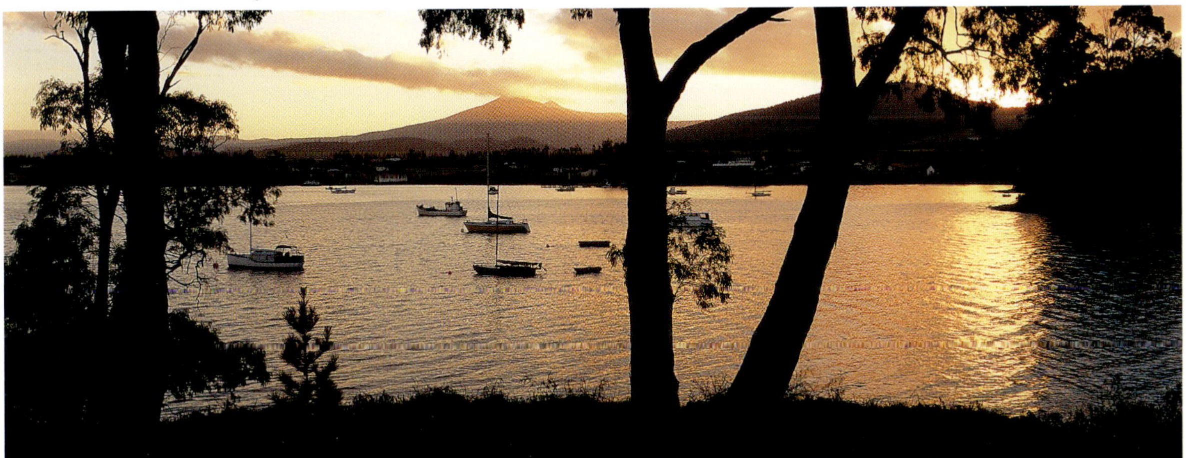

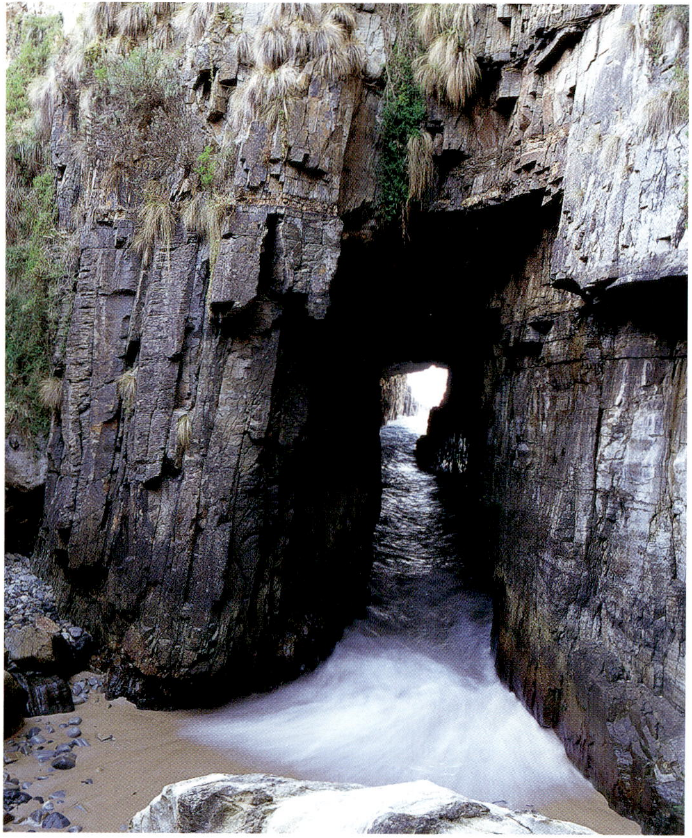

Remarkable Cave about 10 minutes from Port Arthur.

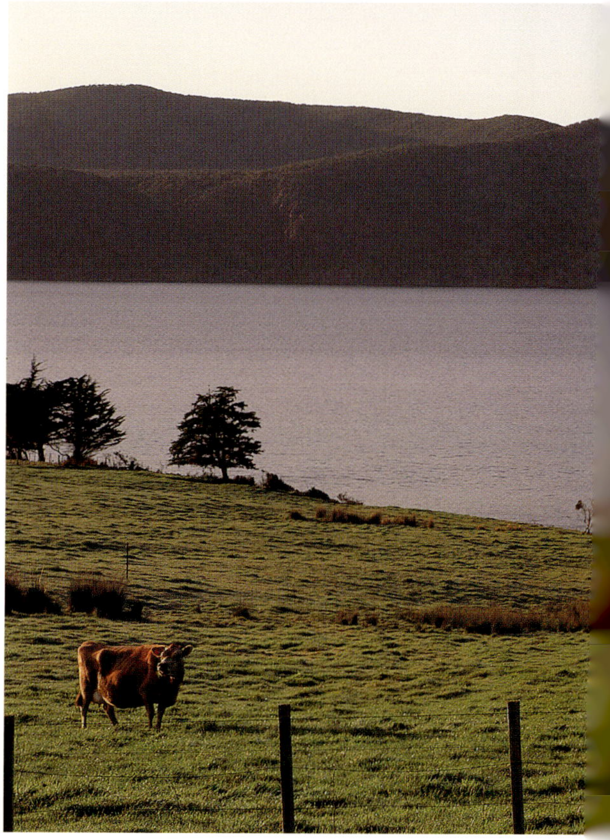

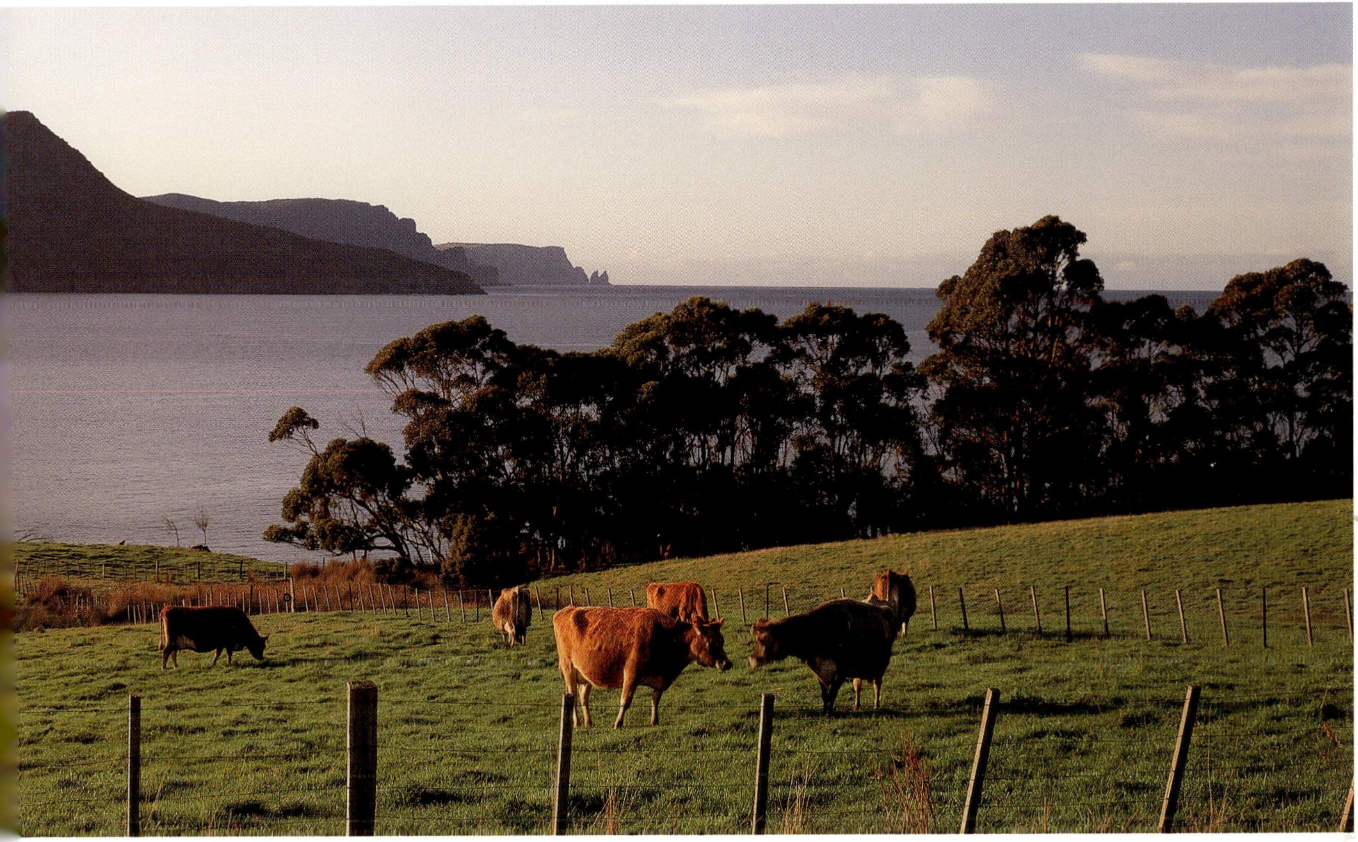

Safety Cove on the Tasman Peninsula near Port Arthur. Tasman Island is in the background.

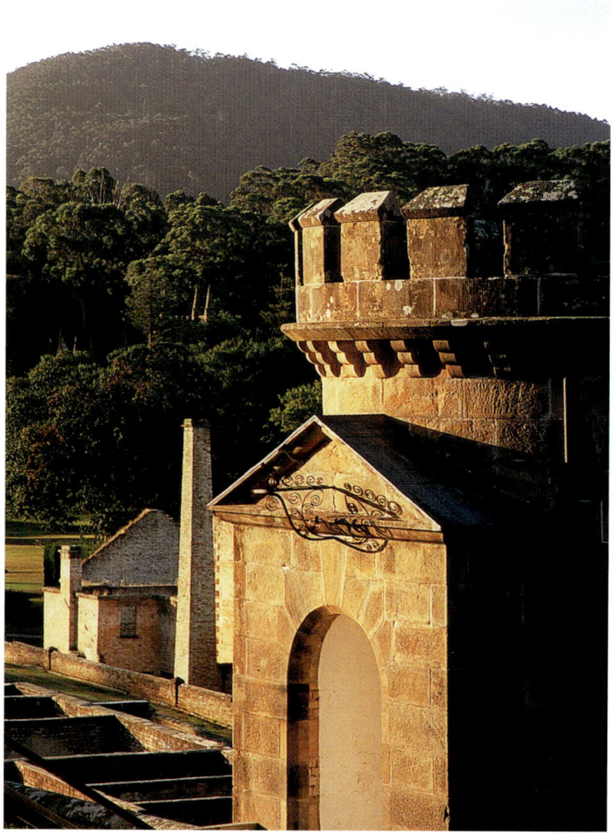

Guard Tower, Port Arthur.

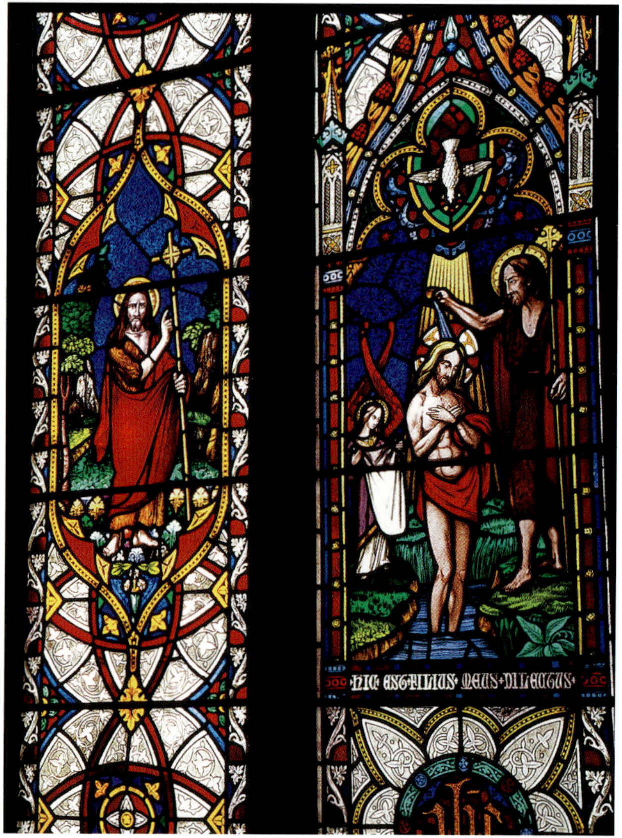

The window of St. John the Baptist church at Buckland

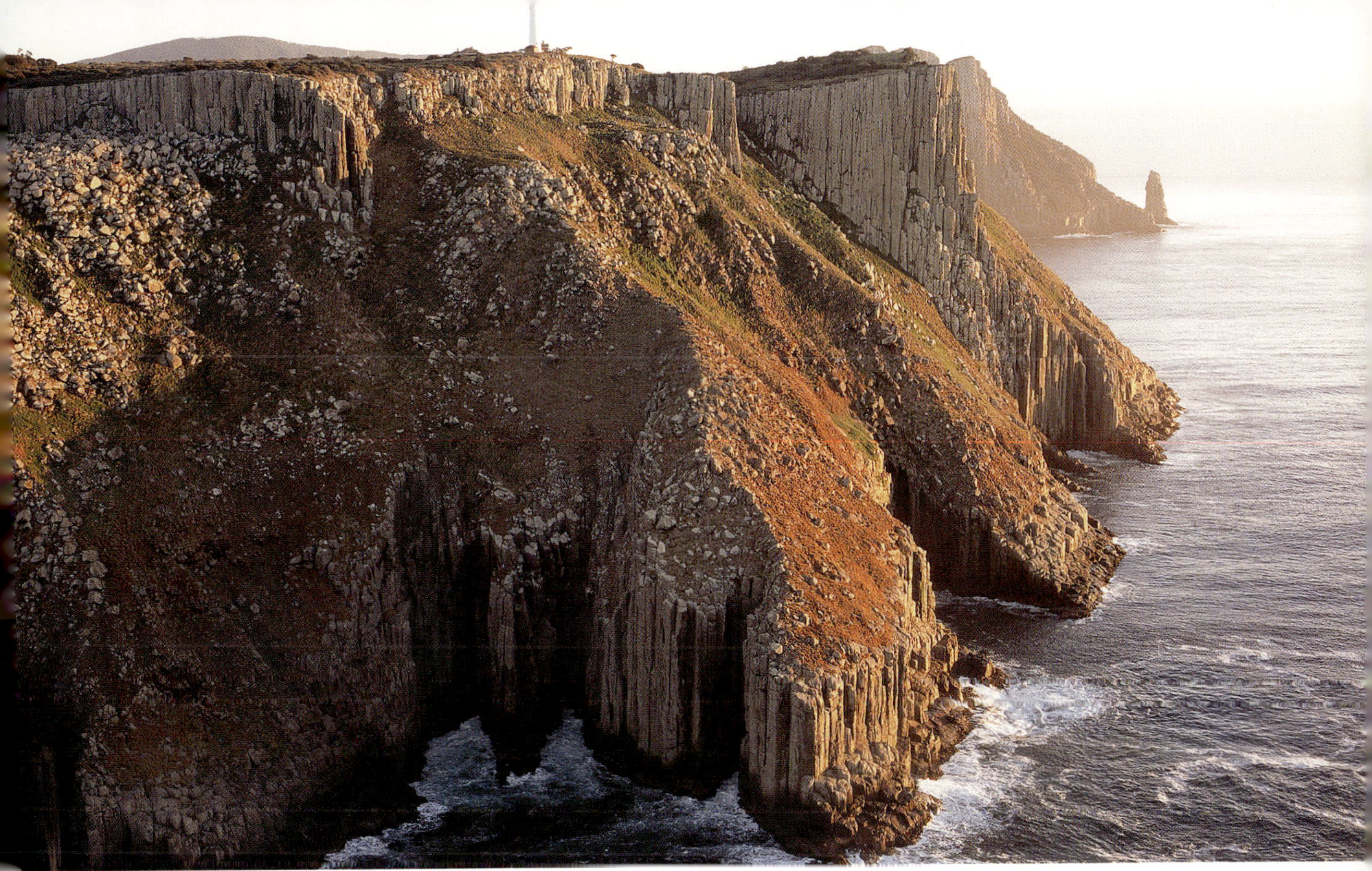

Early morning light on Tasman Island with a glimpse of Cape Pillar behind, in the Tasman National Park.

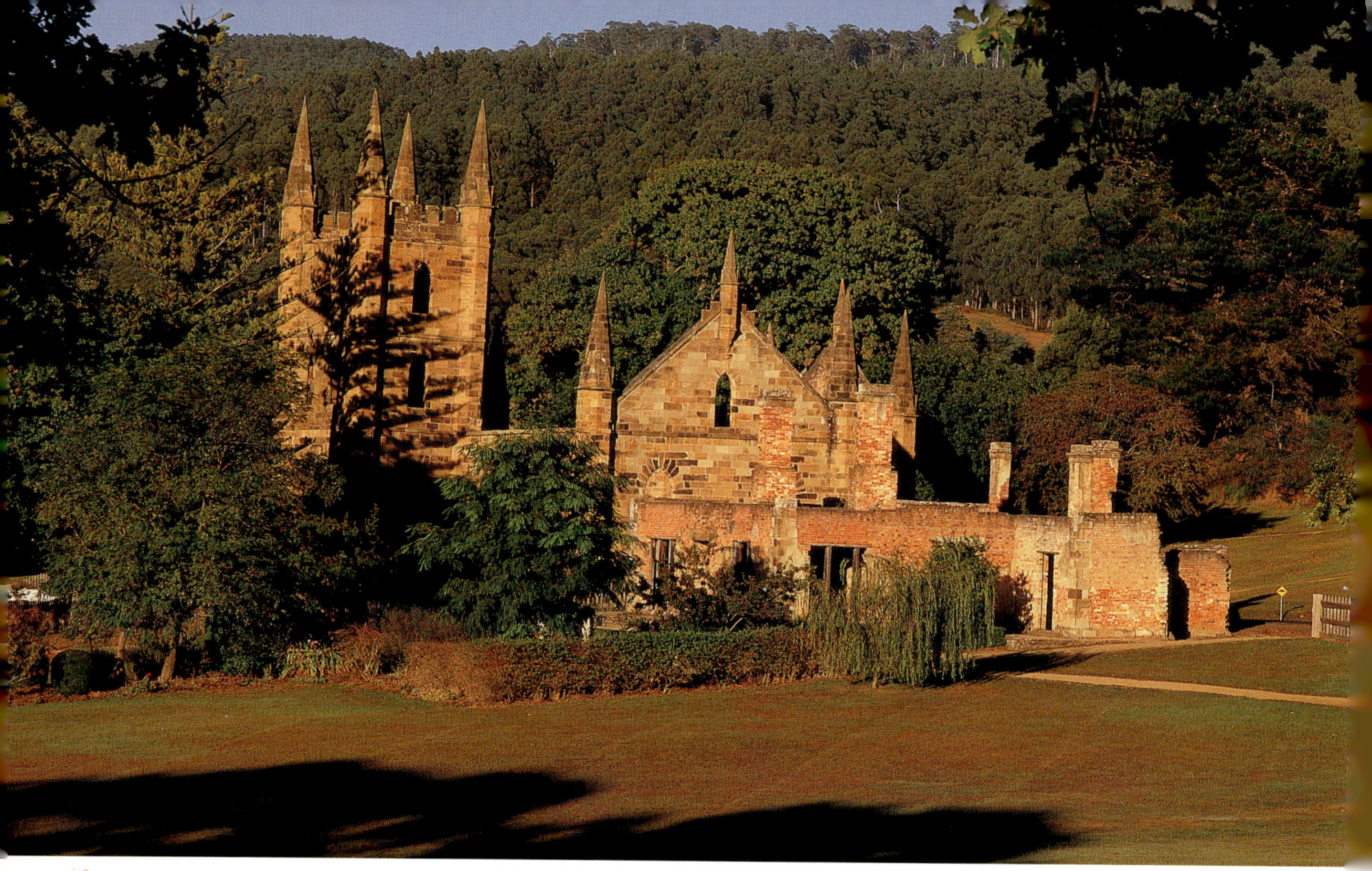

The Church at Port Arthur.

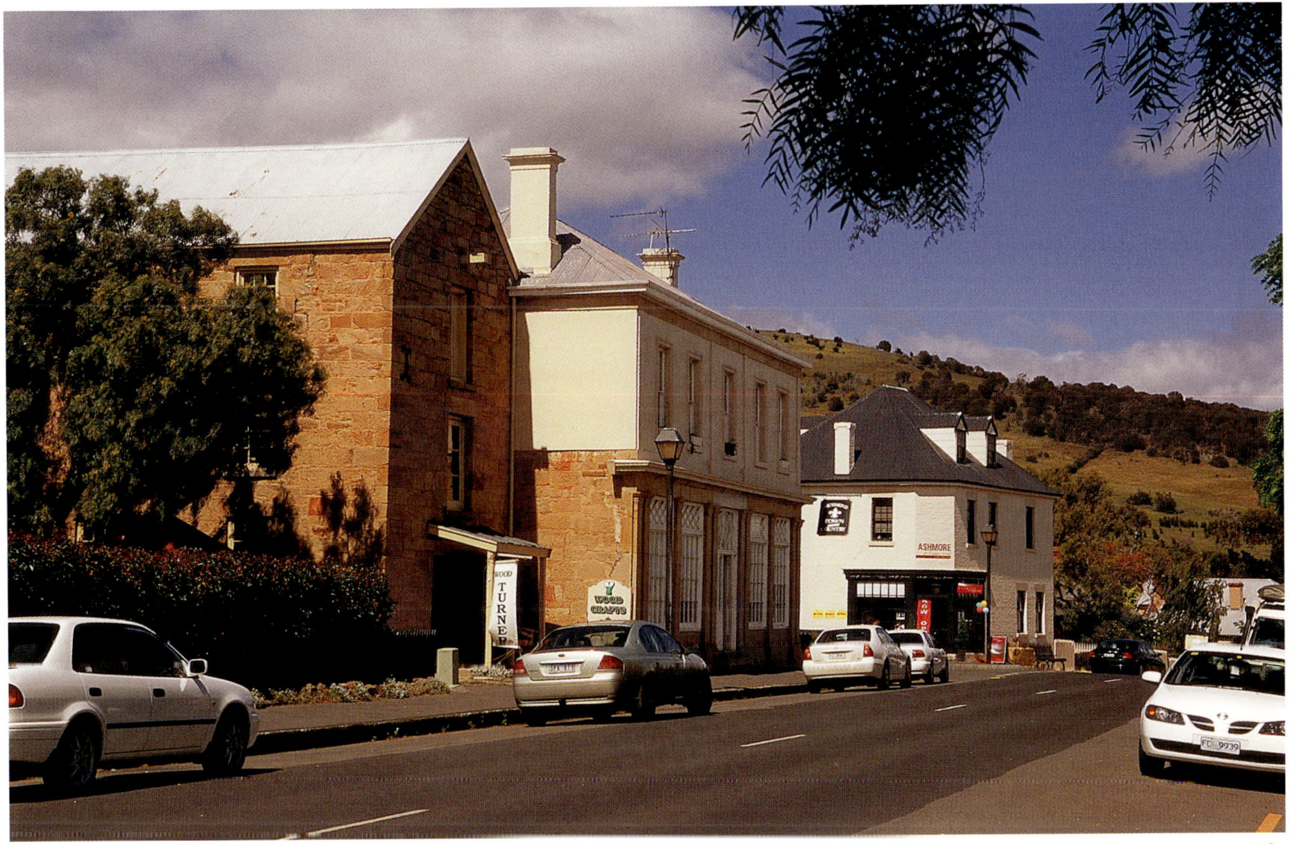

The historic town of Richmond is about 30 minutes from Hobart.

THE NORTH

Despite being the second largest city in Tasmania, Launceston is the trade and tourism centre of the State.

Bell Bay, close to where the original settlement was made by William Paterson at York Town in 1804, is the major port.

The site for Launceston 60km inland from the mouth of the Tamar River was eventually picked because of its superior agricultural potential.

It quickly became the hub of a thriving farming industry which spread south to the Midlands, west towards Deloraine and north-east toward Scottsdale.

Because of its geographically central position, Launceston is a popular starting and finishing point for tourists.

It is situated at the confluence of the South and North Esk rivers and much further inland than all other major cities.

Launceston has a vast array of attractions well suited to day trips.

The closest and easily the most popular is the Cataract Gorge and First Basin Reserve situated a few minutes walk from the centre of the city.

About the turn of this century a walkway was built along the side of the Gorge and a suspension bridge was built across the South Esk at the head of the First Basin.

The area around Launceston is dotted with many historically classified towns and magnificent Victorian and Georgian mansions.

Longford and Evandale are just 20 minutes drive from Launceston and further south along the Heritage Highway are the towns of Campbell Town and Ross. All boast of many historic buildings, bridges and statues.

To the north there are also many historic and picturesque attractions including a wealth of boutique wineries, apple orchards, gold mining museum, Platypus House, Sea Horse World and the Swiss village of Grindelwald.

Near the mouth of the Tamar River are George Town and Low Head where the pilot station and Low Head lighthouse are open for inspection. Also not to be missed is the seaside holiday and fishing town of Bridport and the rich farming district of Scottsdale.

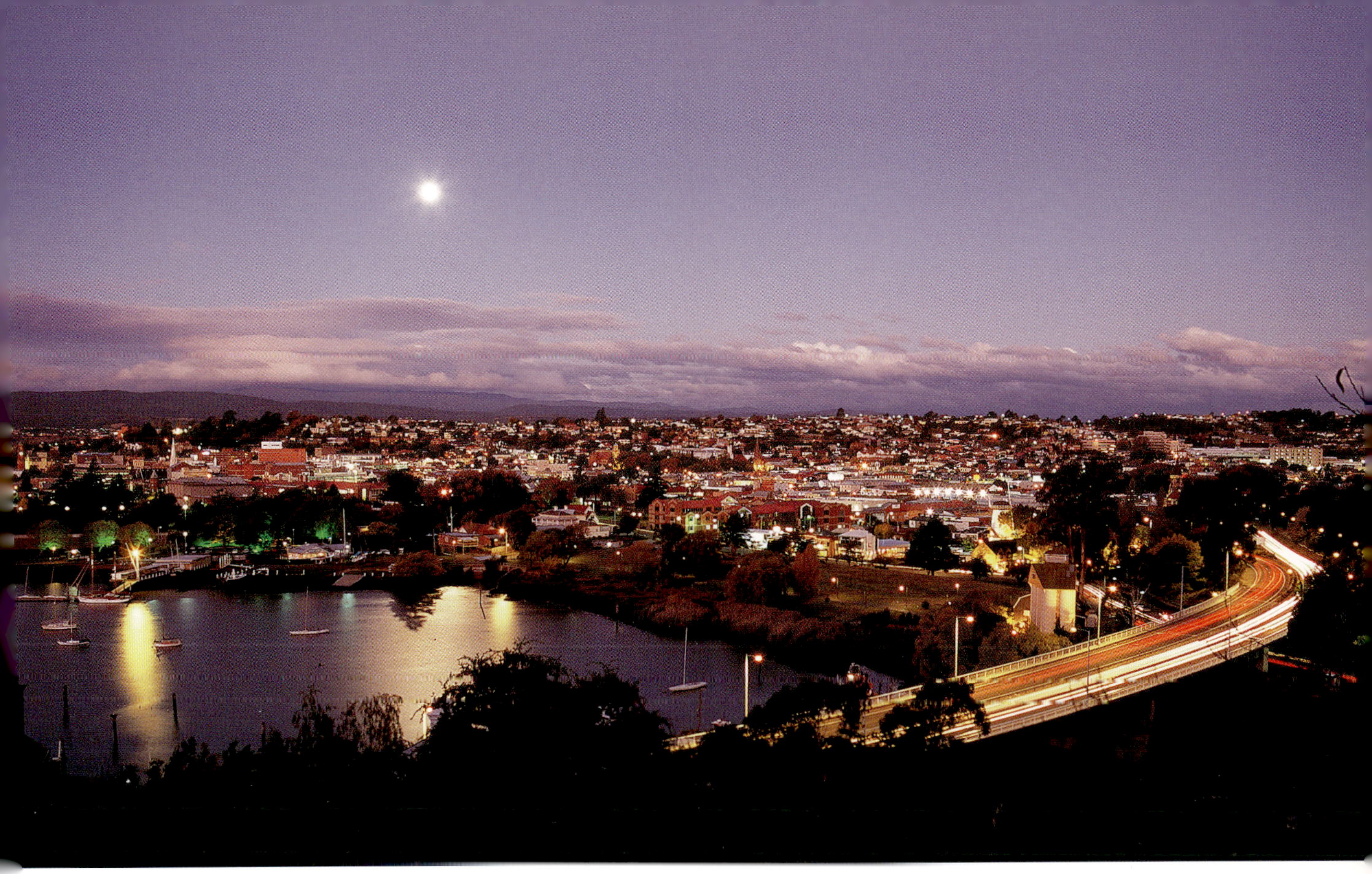

Full moon over the city of Launceston and the Tamar River.

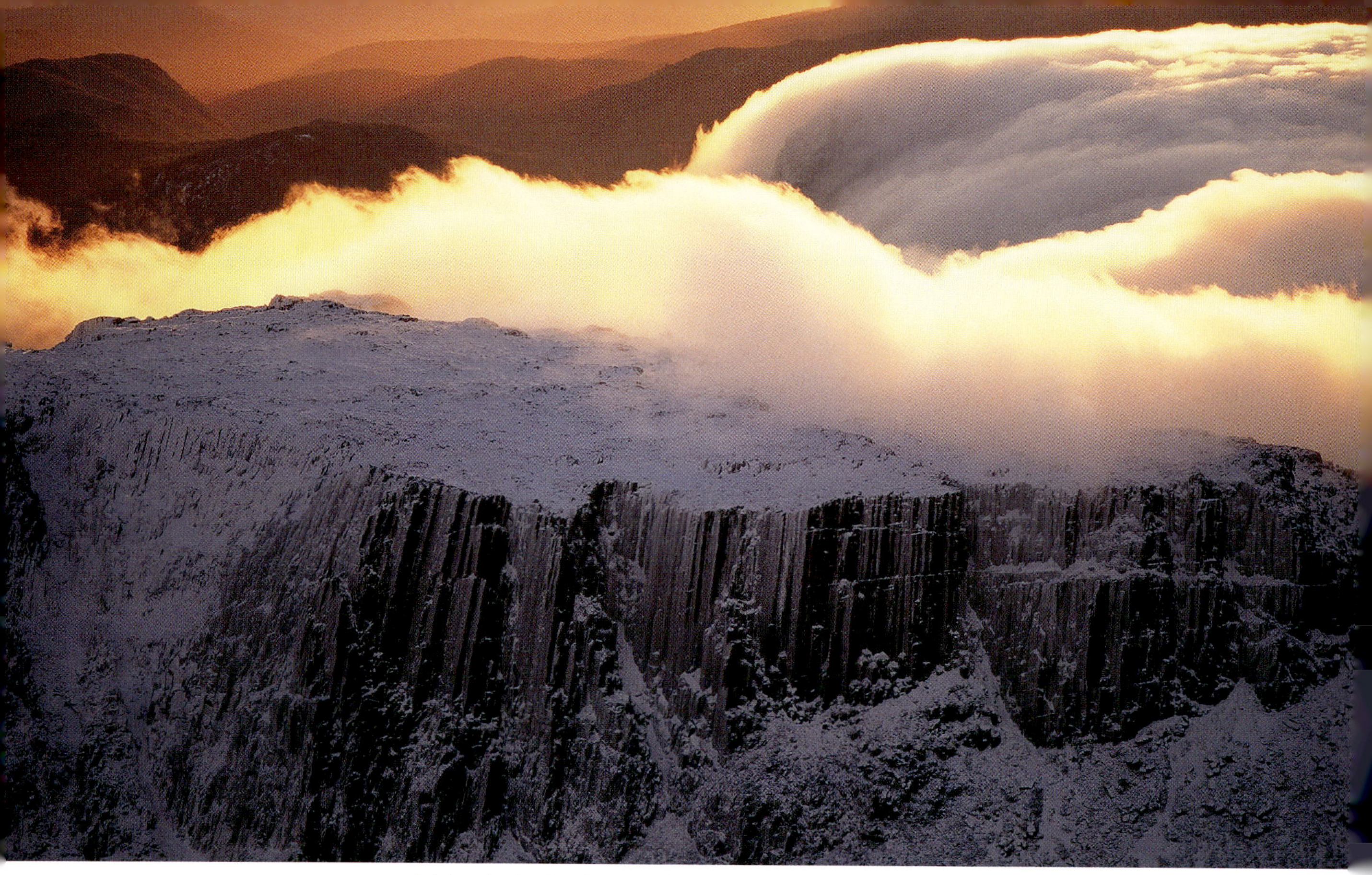

A blanket of mist settles over Ben Lomond.

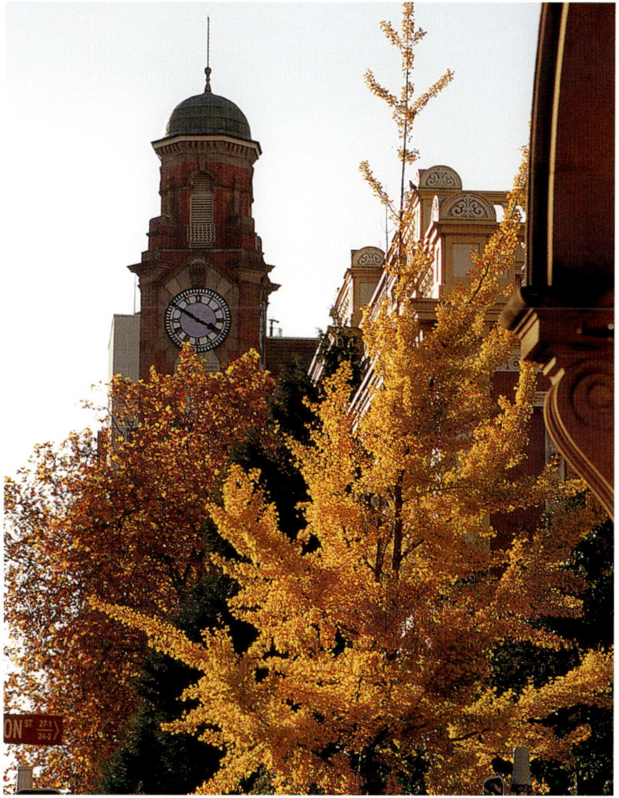

Launceston town clock and public buildings.

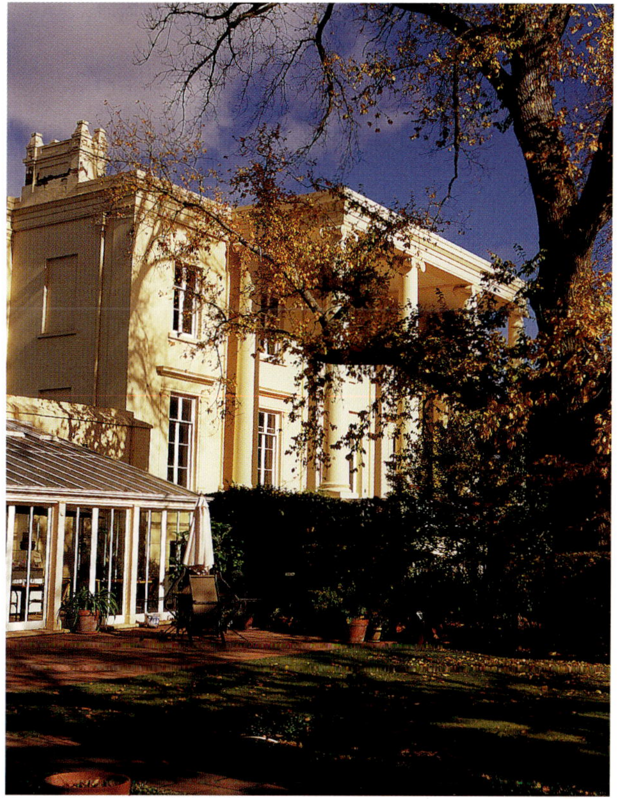

Historic Clarendon homestead at Nile.

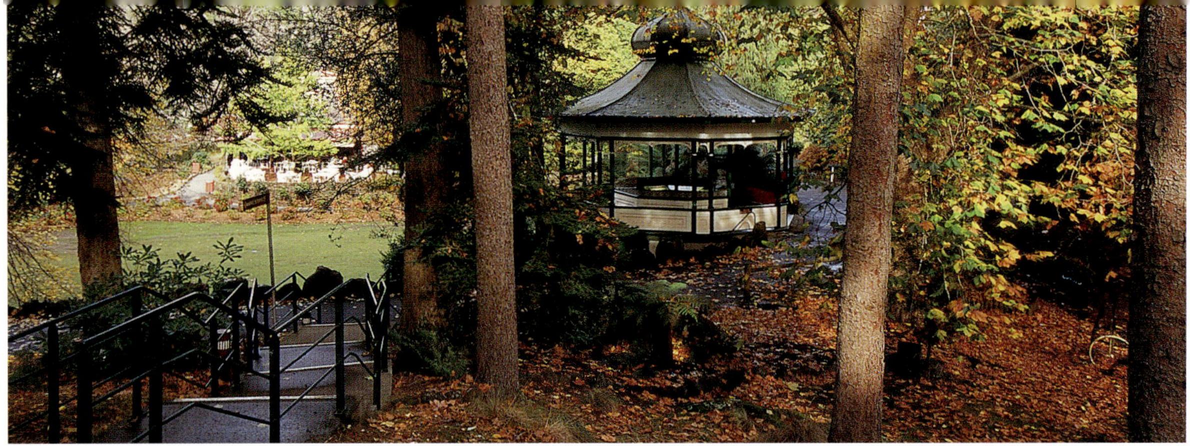

The Cataract Gorge gardens, Launceston

The Cataract Gorge in flood.

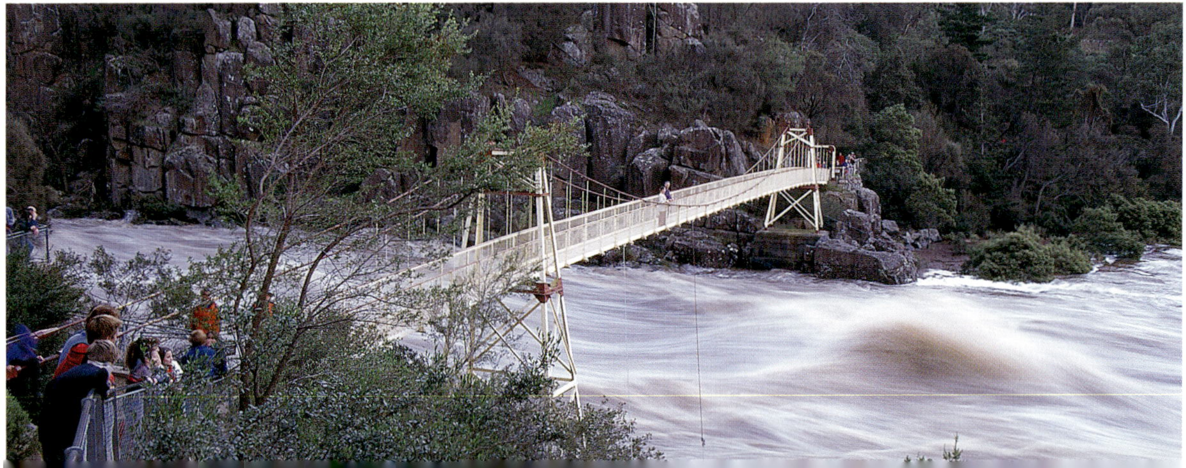

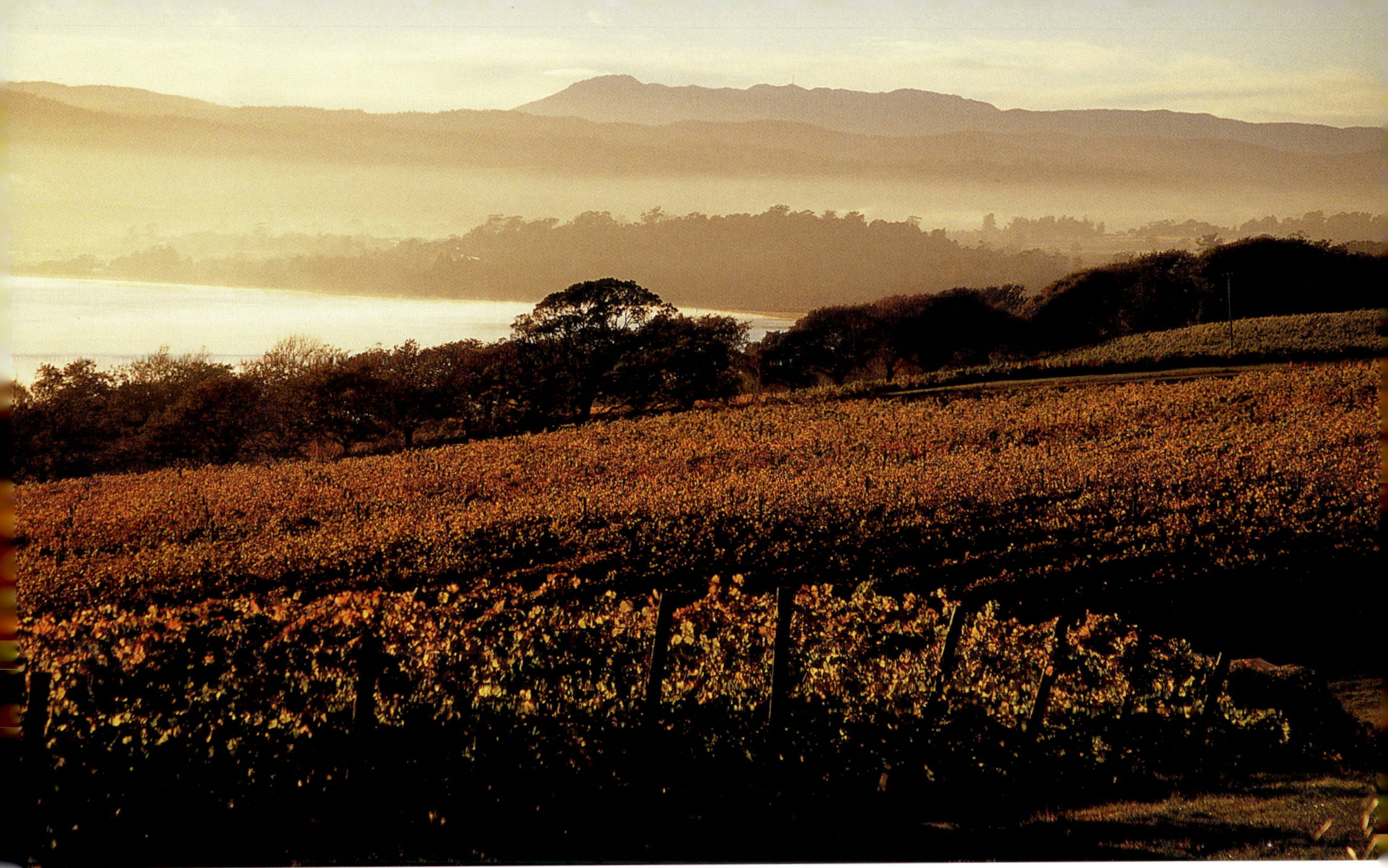

Autumn mist at Rosevears where several boutique wineries line the banks of the Tamar River.

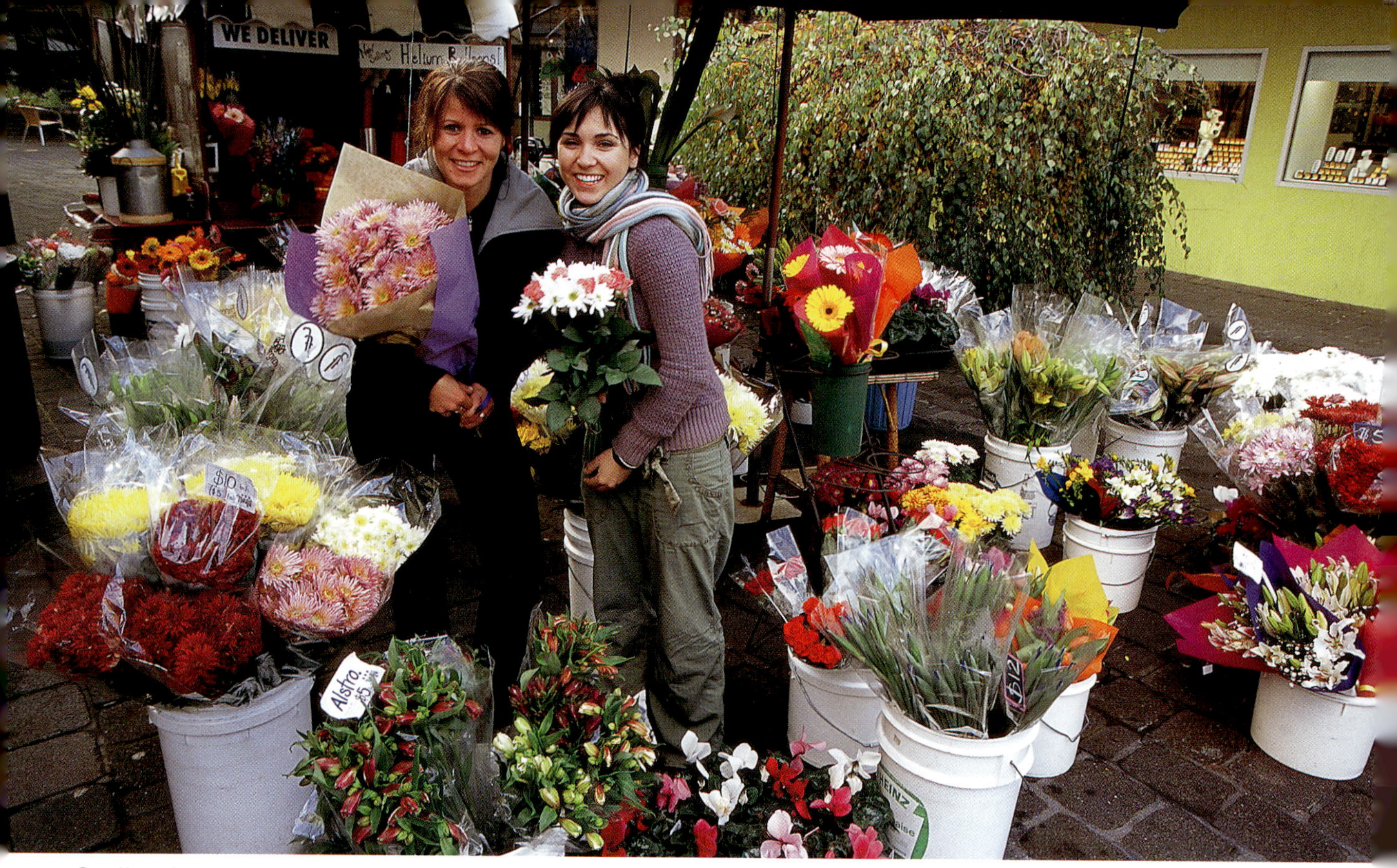

Smiles from the Quadrant Mall flower barrow girls, Nicola Kurth and Angela Rushby, Launceston.

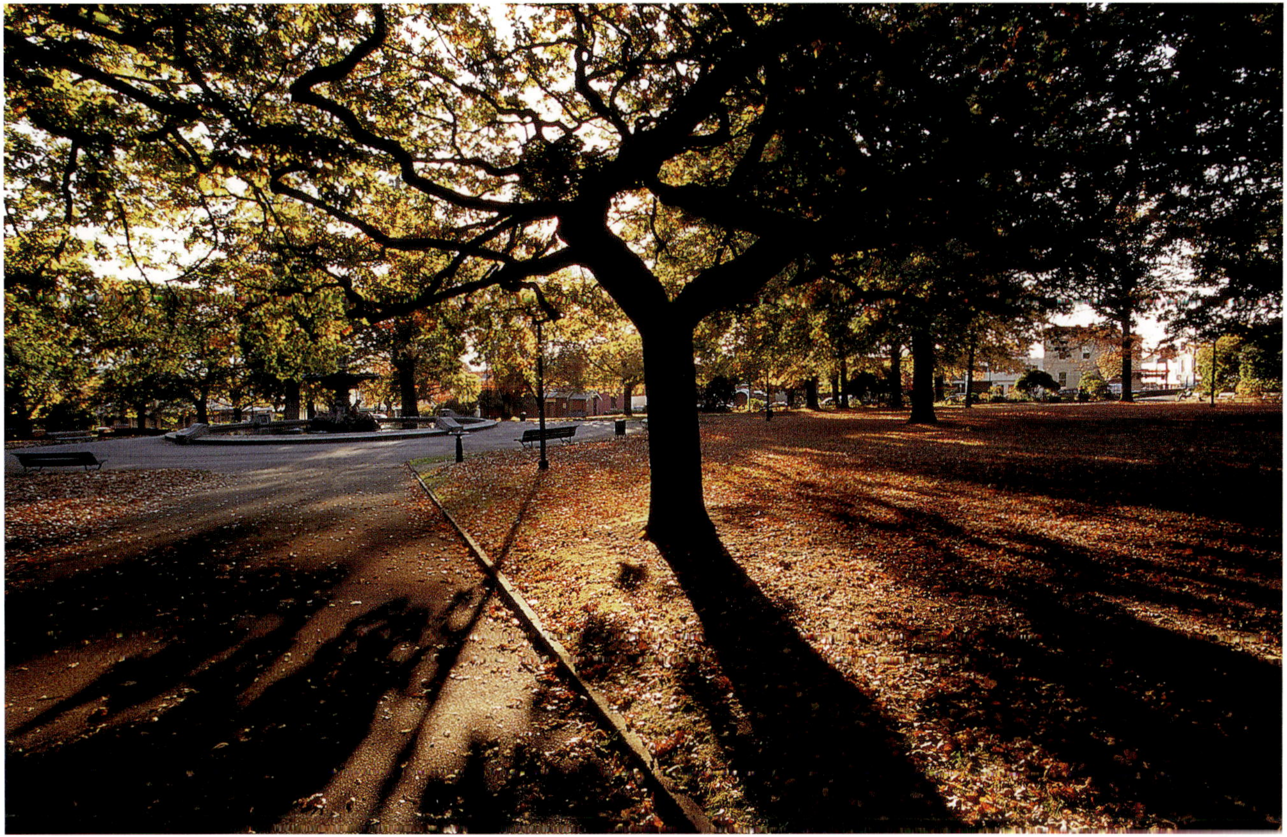

Autumn light on Princes Square, Launceston.

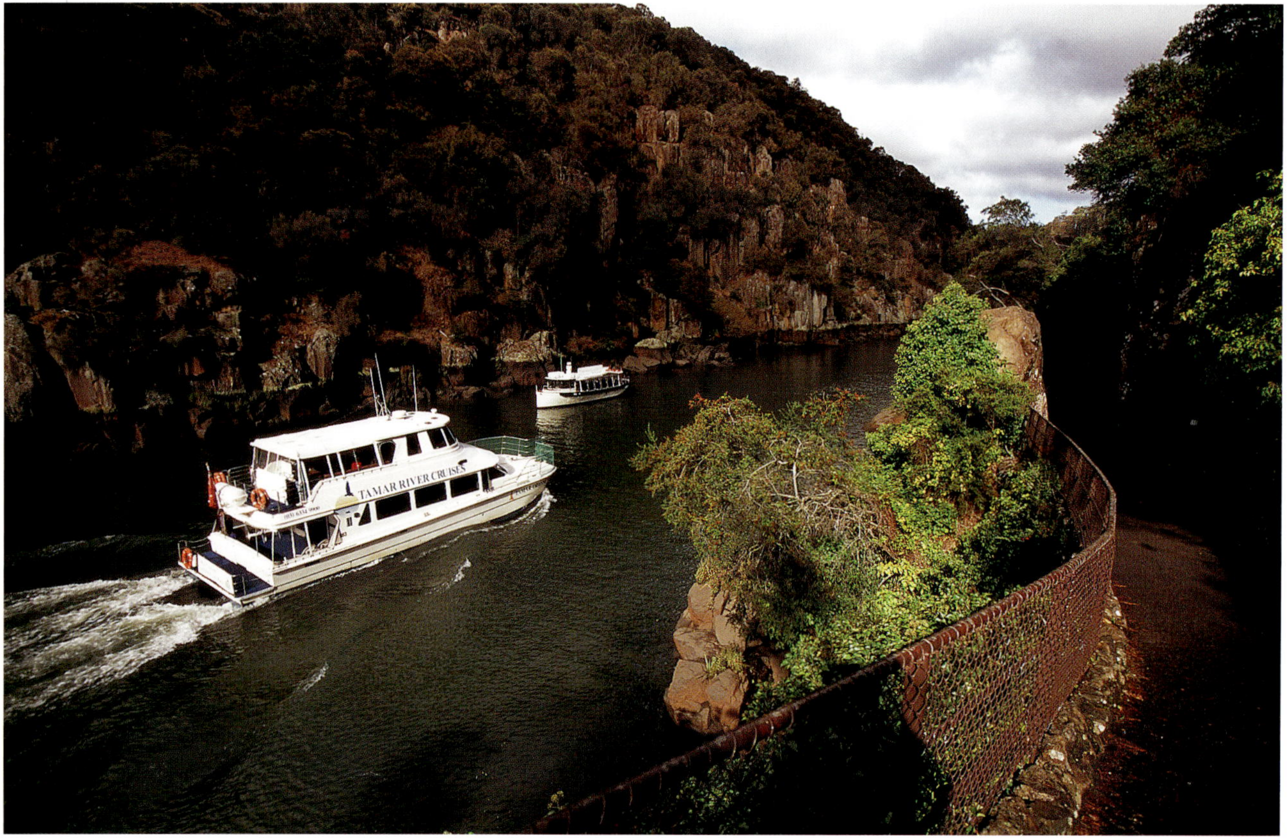

Tamar River Cruises boats 'Tamar Odyssey' and 'Lady Launceston' in Launceston's Cataract Gorge.

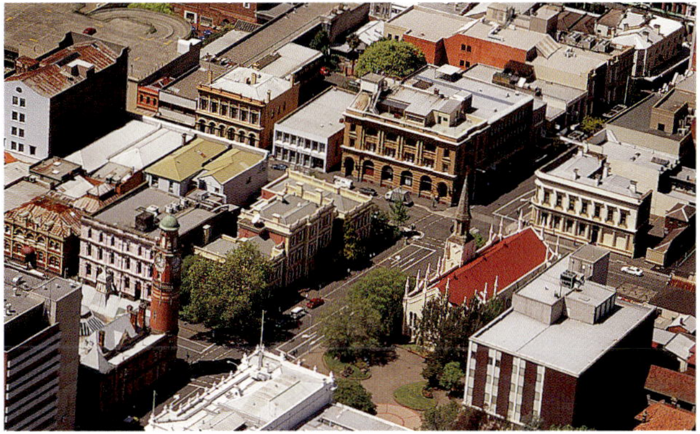

Historic buildings, Launceston.

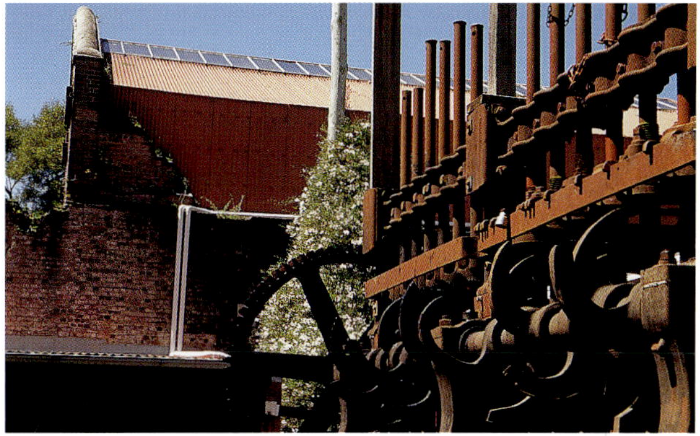

Grubb Shaft Museum, Beaconsfield.

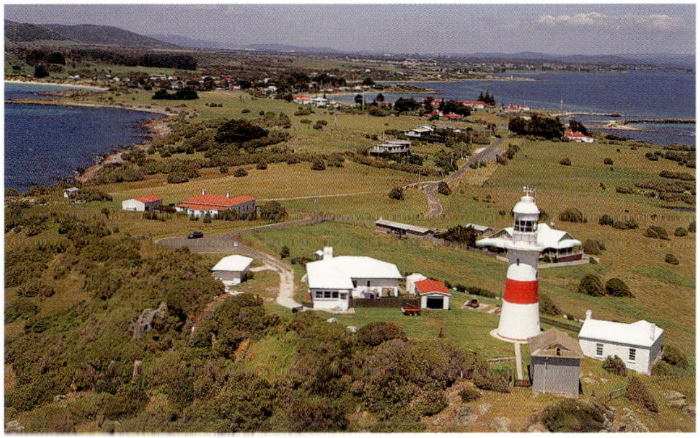

Low Head lighthouse

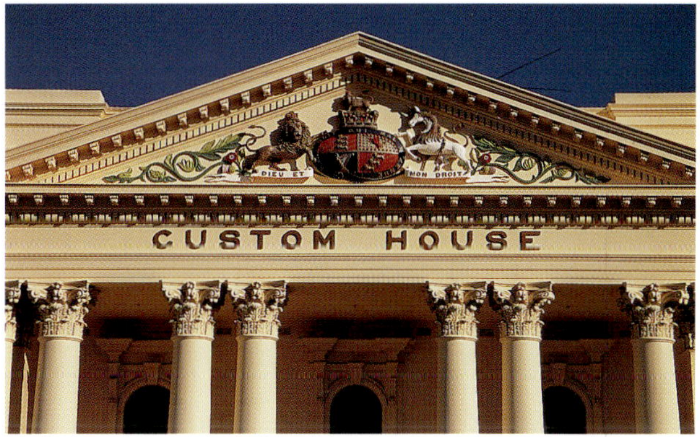

Custom House (1897), Launceston.

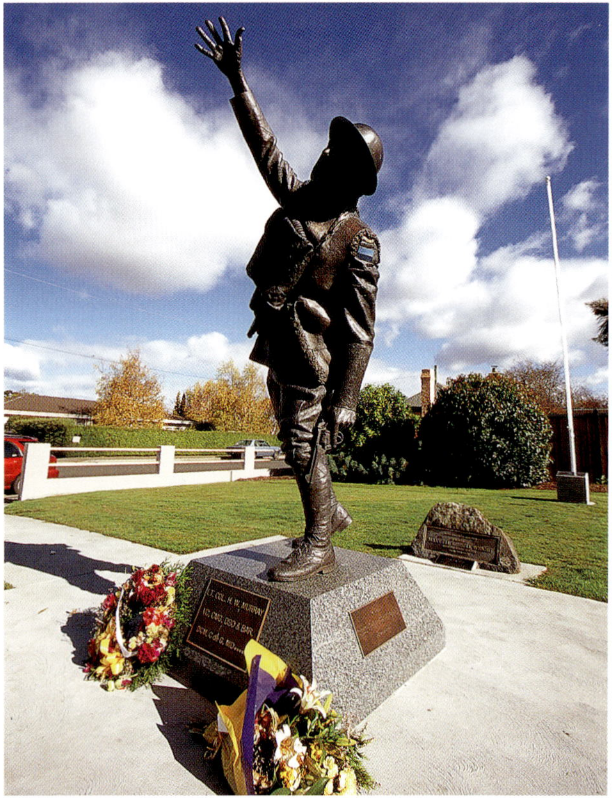

The statue at Evandale of Australia's most decorated soldier, Harry Murray.

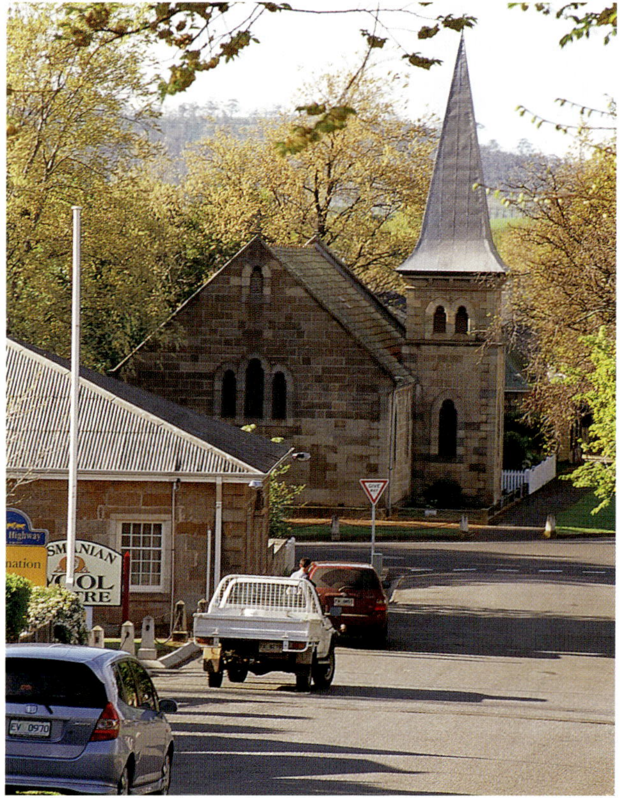

Historic town of Ross on the Heritage Highway.

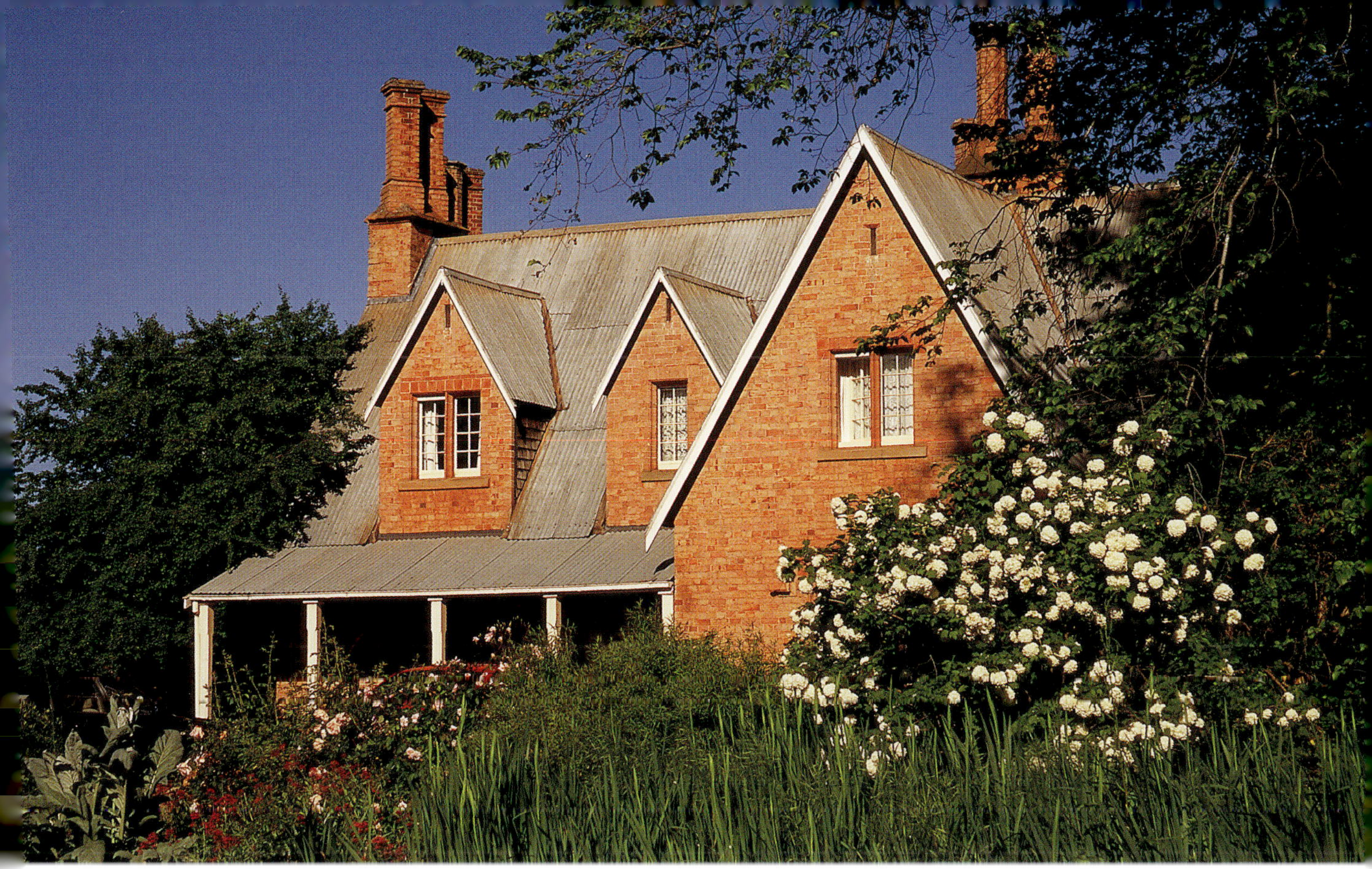

The Grange Conference Centre at Campbell Town on the Heritage Highway about 70 kms. south of Launceston.

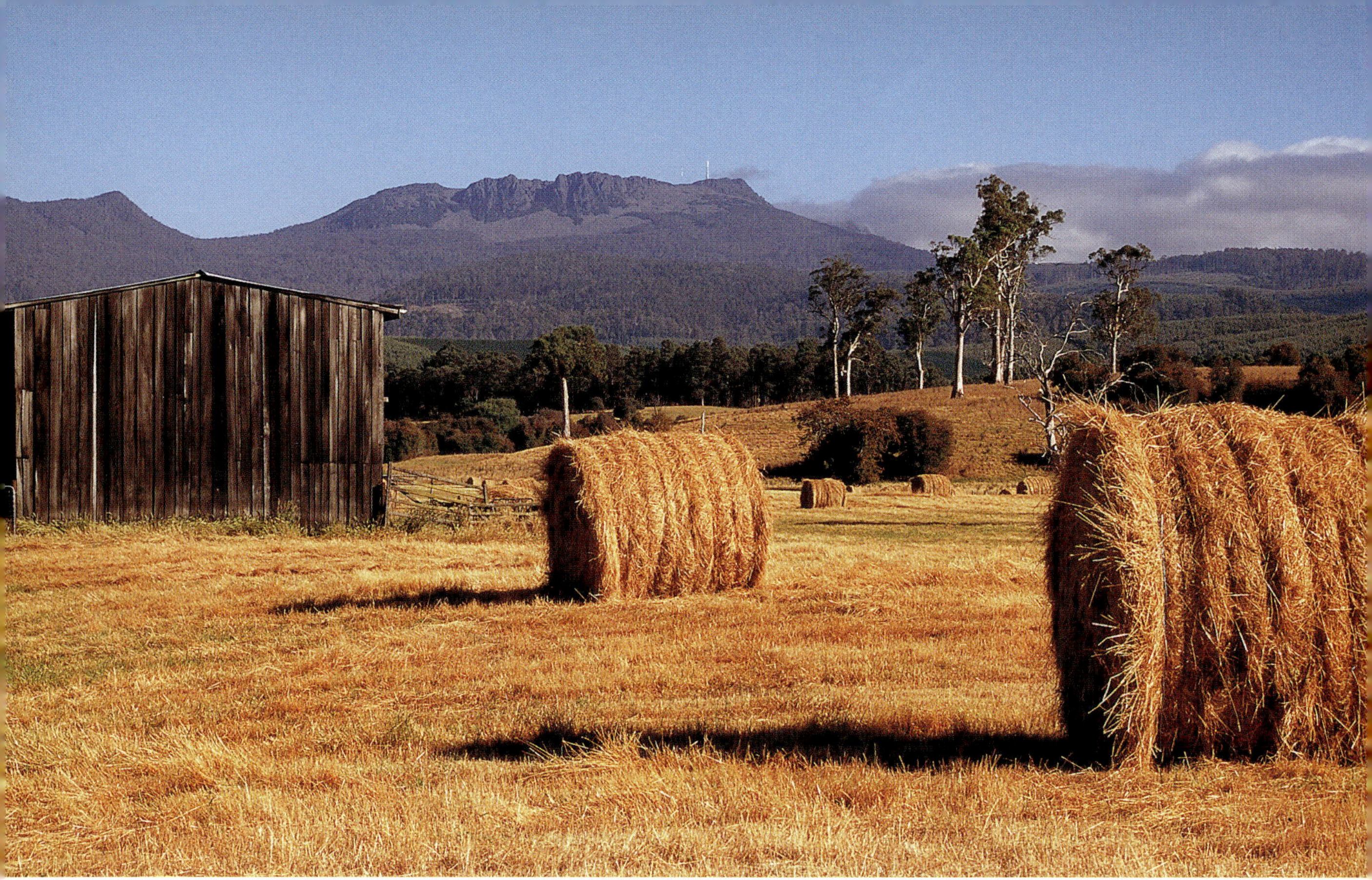

Mt. Barrow is the backdrop to hay making time at Blessington.

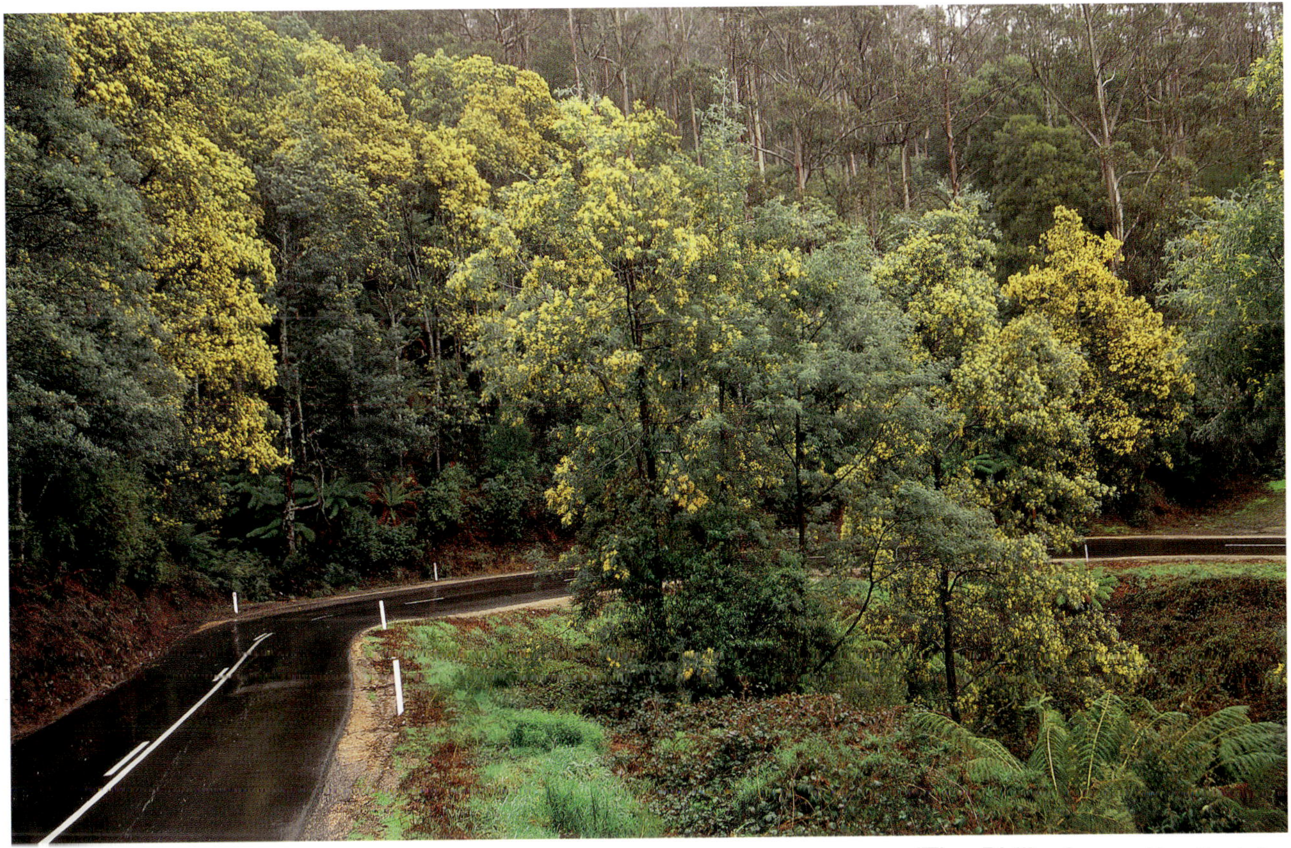

The Tasman Highway winds through spring-time wattle blossom on 'The Sidling' near Scottsdale.

THE NORTH-WEST and WEST

Primary industry has made Tasmania's North-West and West Coast part of the State's richest areas.

Inland there is a unique treasure in the Cradle Mountain - Lake St. Clair National Park.

Many thousands walk the Cradle Mountain Overland Track each year and it is clearly the State's premier national park.

Two of the principle areas of population along the North-West coast are Devonport and Burnie.

Devonport is also the terminus for the Bass Strait passenger ferries from Melbourne.

Burnie is arguably the commercial centre of the region with several large industries and an outlet for the surrounding primary industries with rail head and port.

Further along the coast is the fascinating township of Stanley below the spectacular rock outcrop, the Nut.

Stanley is almost a town time has forgotten with original cottages with tourism and fishing as the major sources of income.

A former Prime minister of Australia, the late Joseph Lyons, was born at Stanley and his cottage is well marked.

The discovery of alluvial gold led miners to the West Coast settlement of Queenstown which supported 14 hotels at one stage.

Strahan is the starting point for the famous Gordon River cruises and a view of Sarah Island, the State's first penal prison and the setting for Marcus Clarke's novel 'For the Term of His Natural Life'.

Although the level of mining on the West Coast is decreasing, the stark mountains of Queenstown and Museums in Zeehan and Strahan have created a new gold mine for visitors.

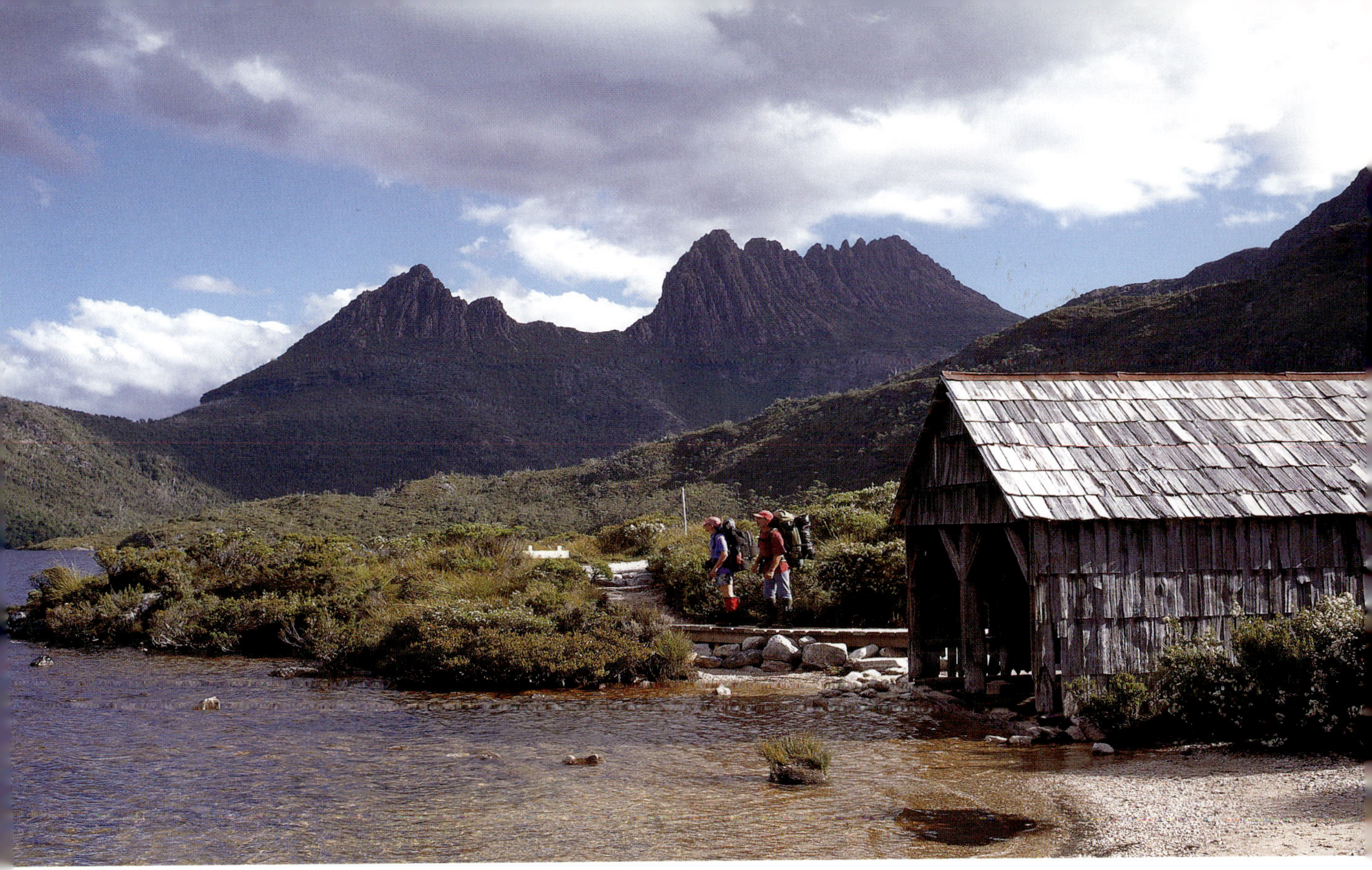

The boat shed at Dove Lake in the Cradle Mountain - Lake St. Clair National Park.

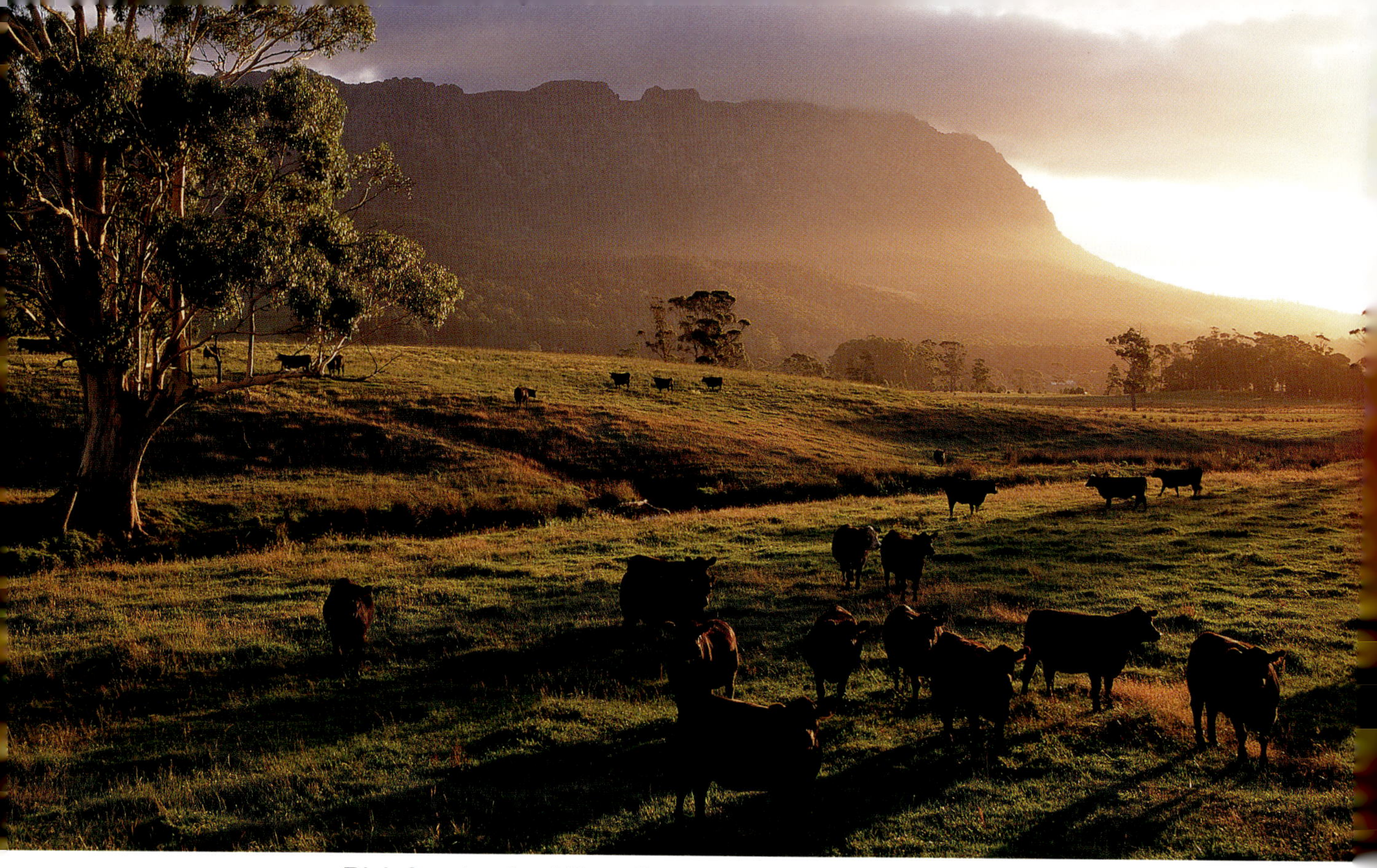

Rich farmlands at Paradise at the foot of Mt. Roland.

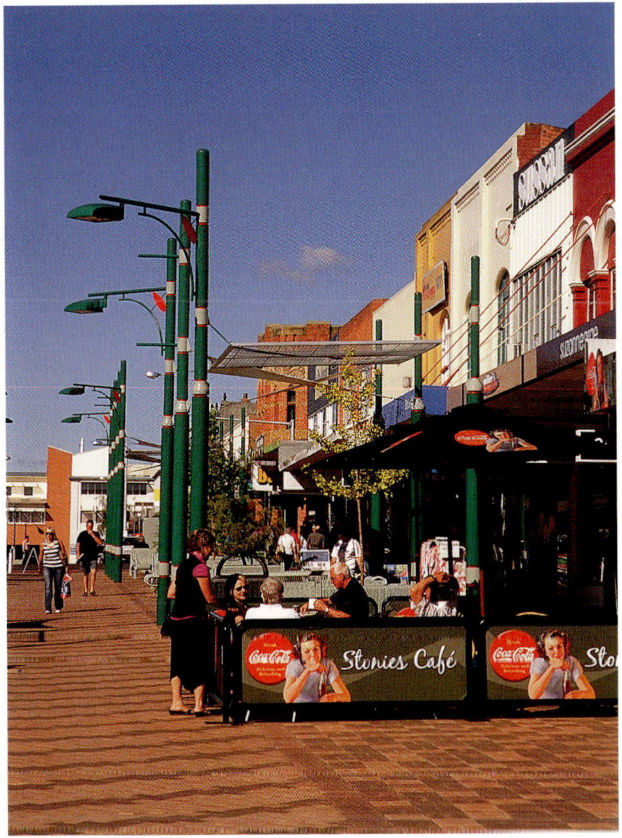

Rooke St. Mall, Devonport.

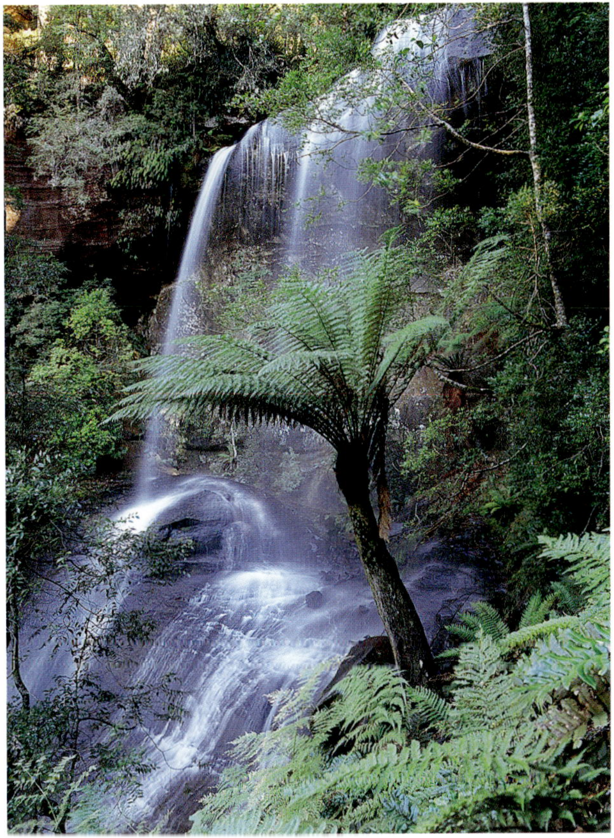

Bridal Veil Falls, Great Western Tiers.

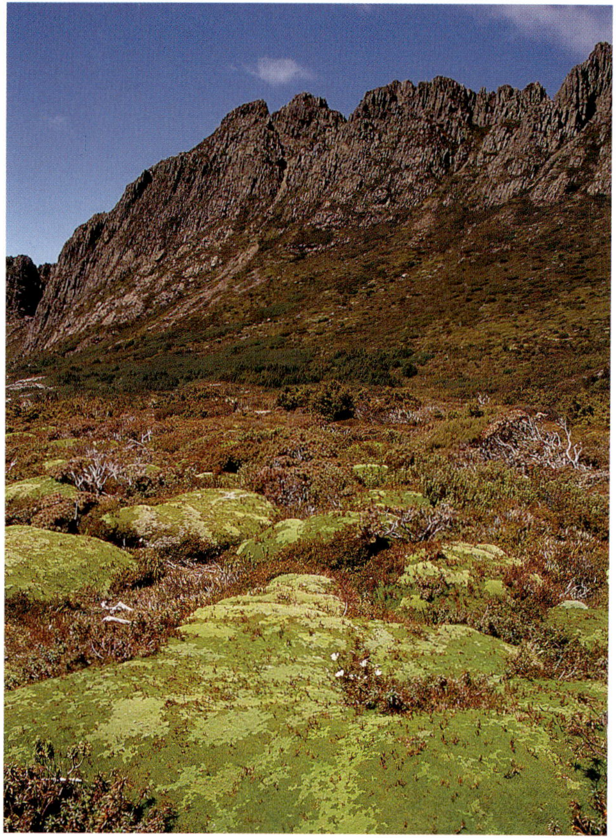

Cushion plants, Cradle Mountain.

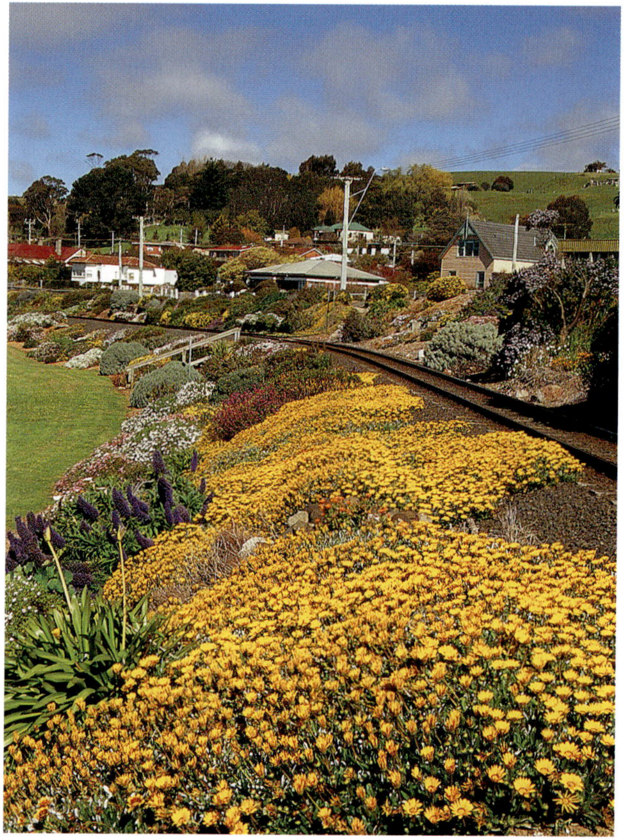

Perry Ling Gardens, Penguin.

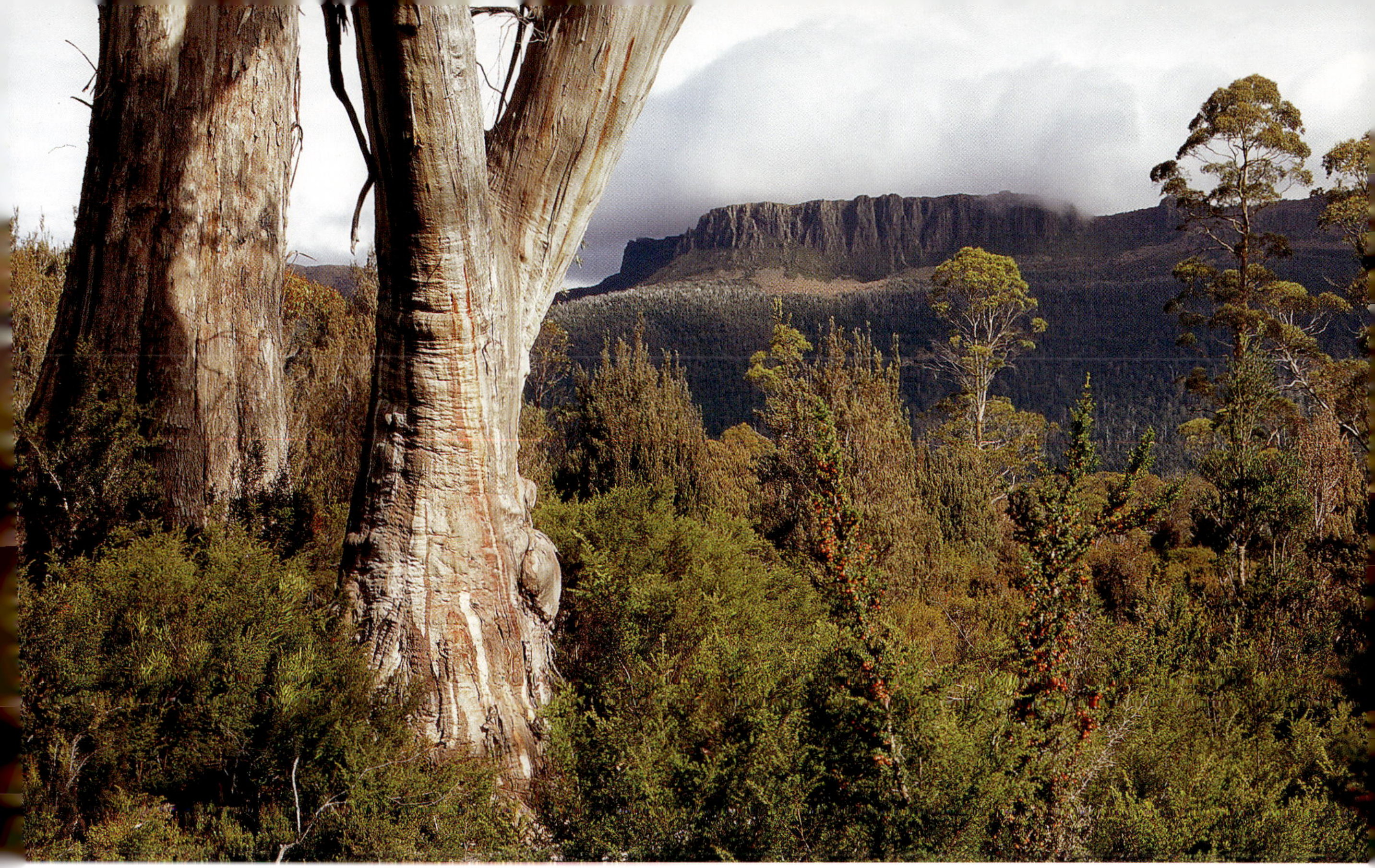

Mt. Olympus in the Cradle Mountain - Lake St. Clair National Park.

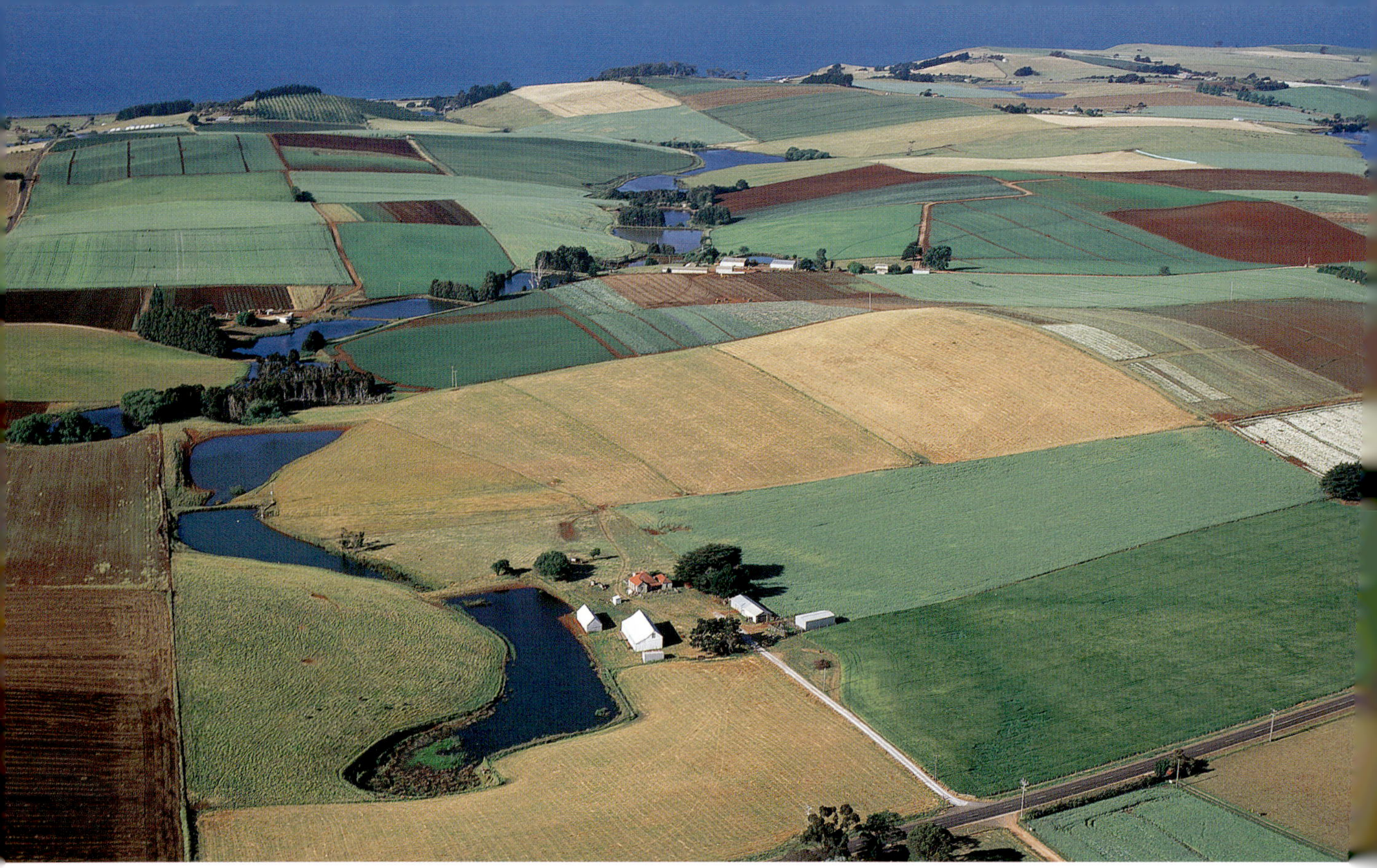

Patchwork farmlands near Devonport where many vegetable crops are grown.

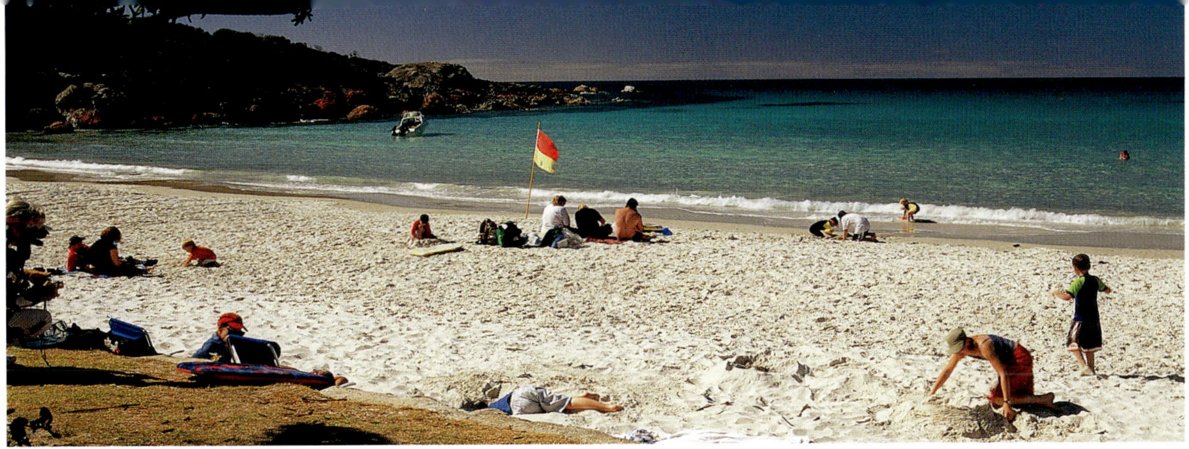

Boat Harbour beach, near Wynyard.

A sea eagle in the Arthur Pieman Conservation Area.

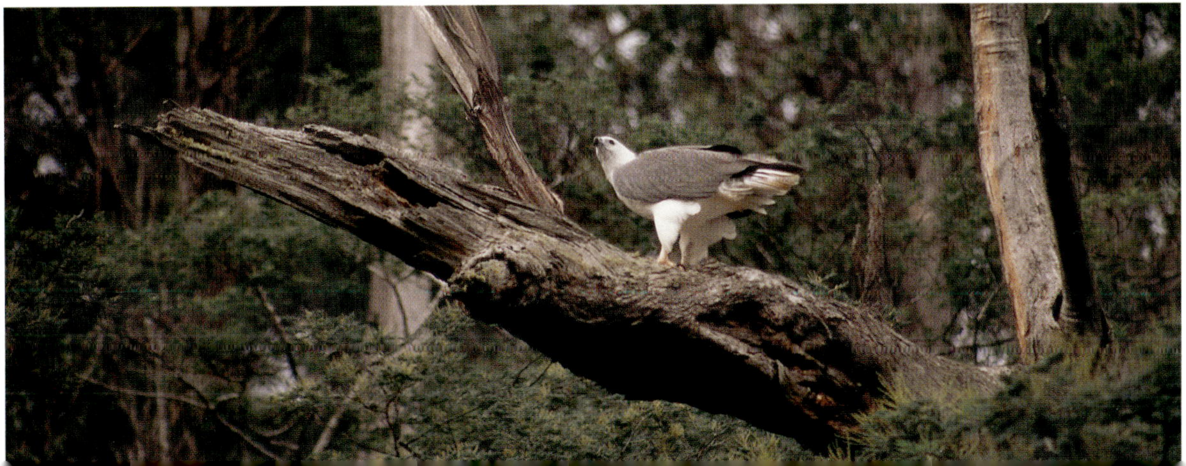

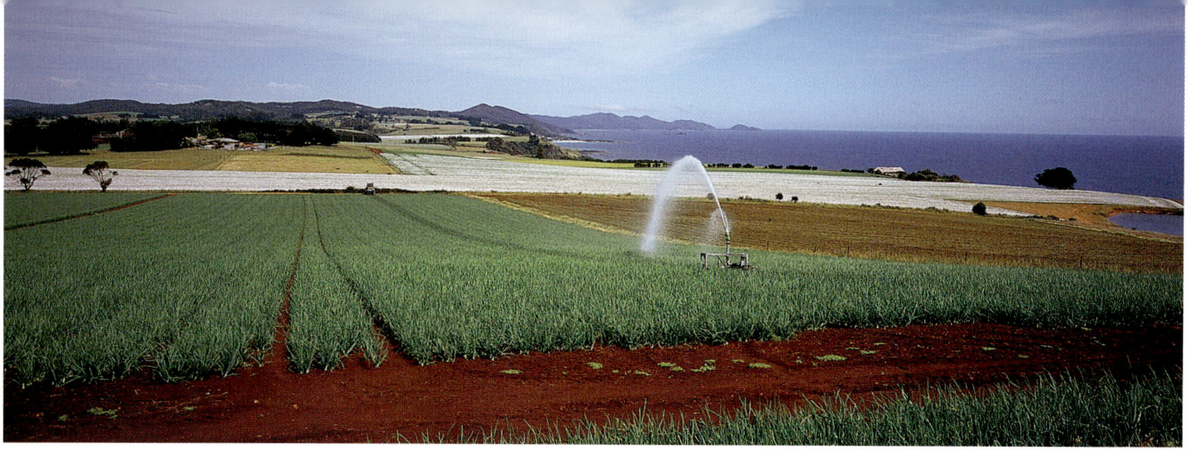

Onions and poppies on Table Cape near Wynyard.

Tulips from Table Cape are exported to Holland and mainland Australia.

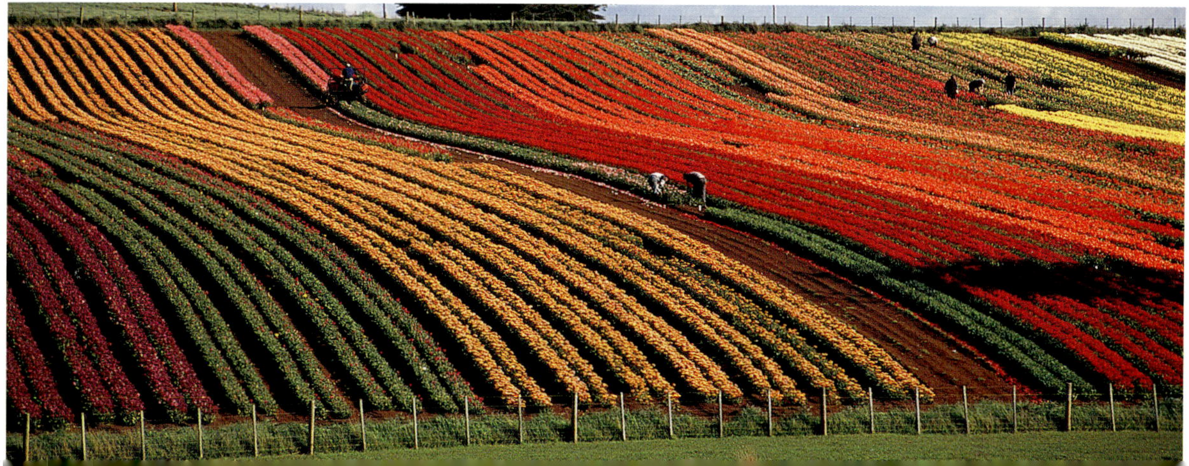

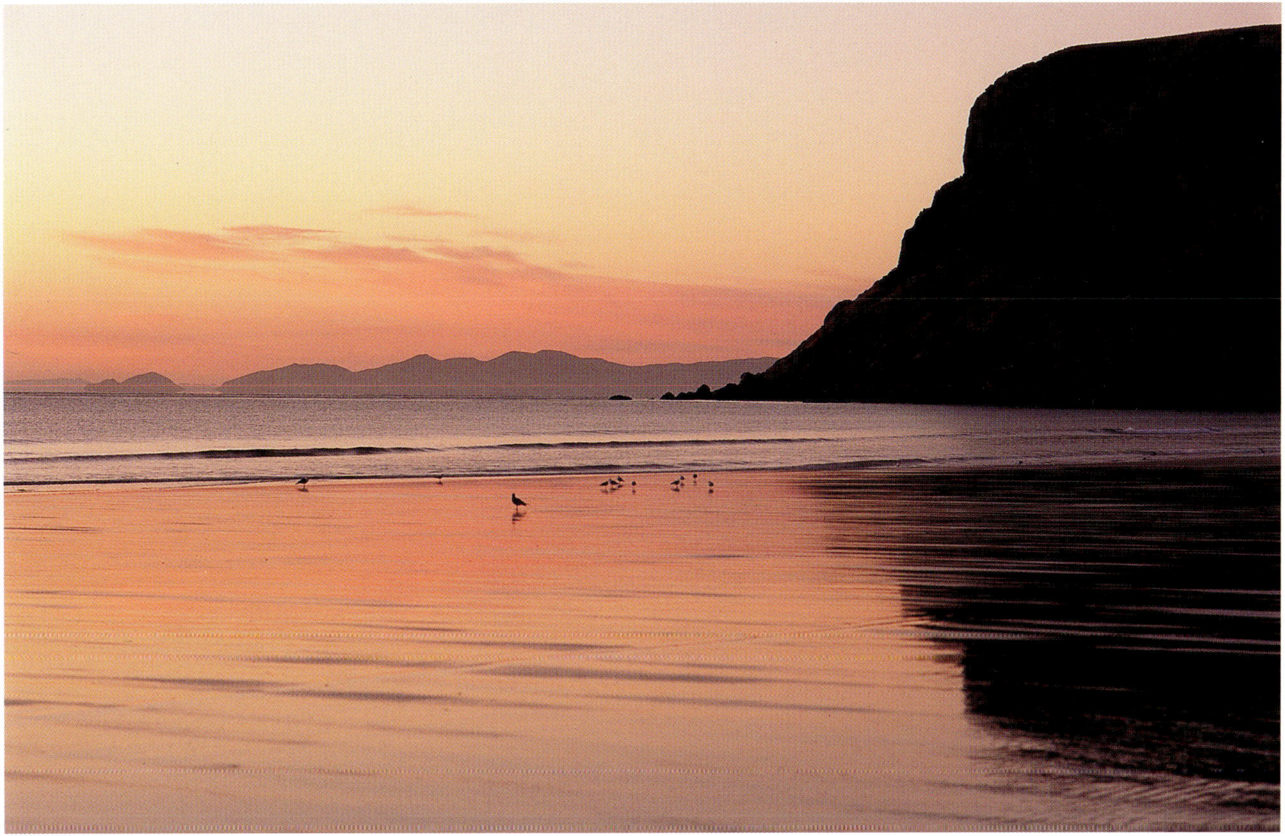

Dawn at Stanley.

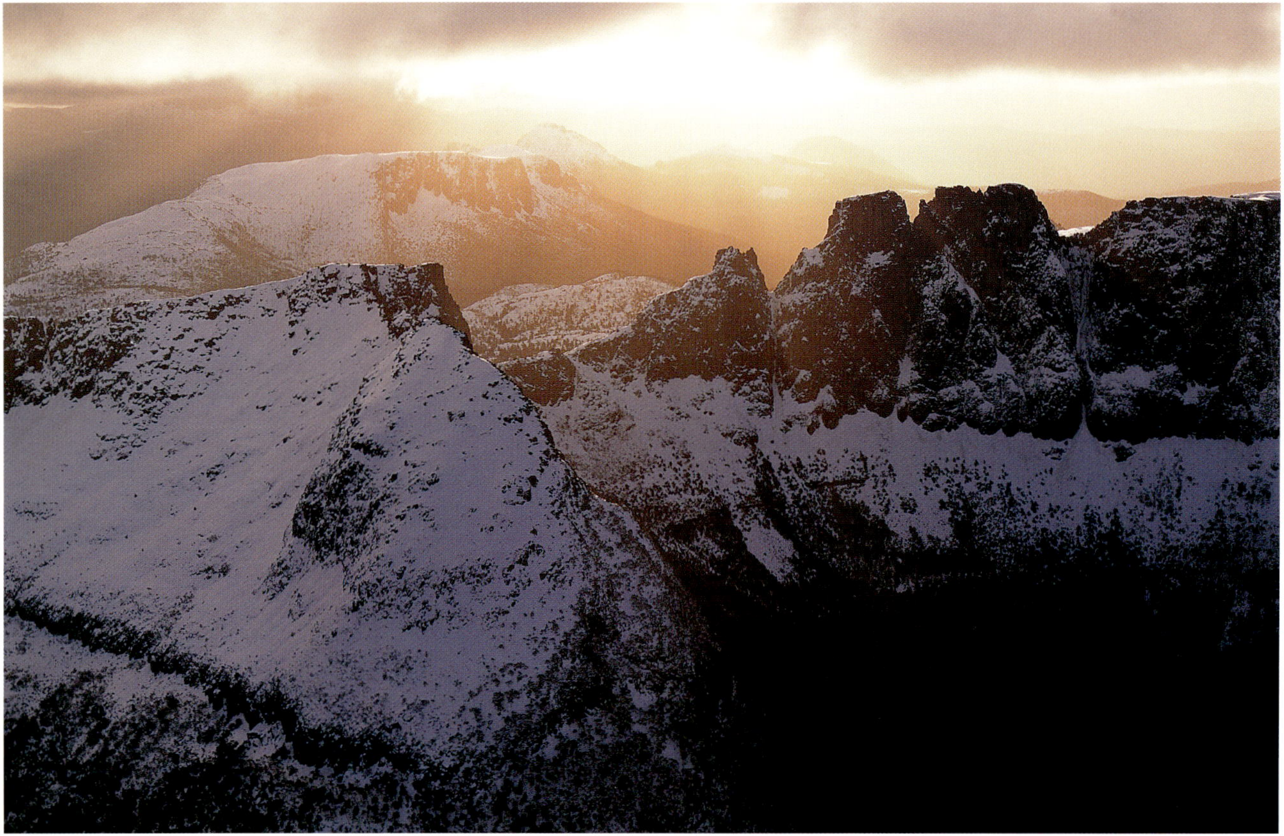

Mt. Geryon, Cradle Mountain - Lake St. Clair National Park.

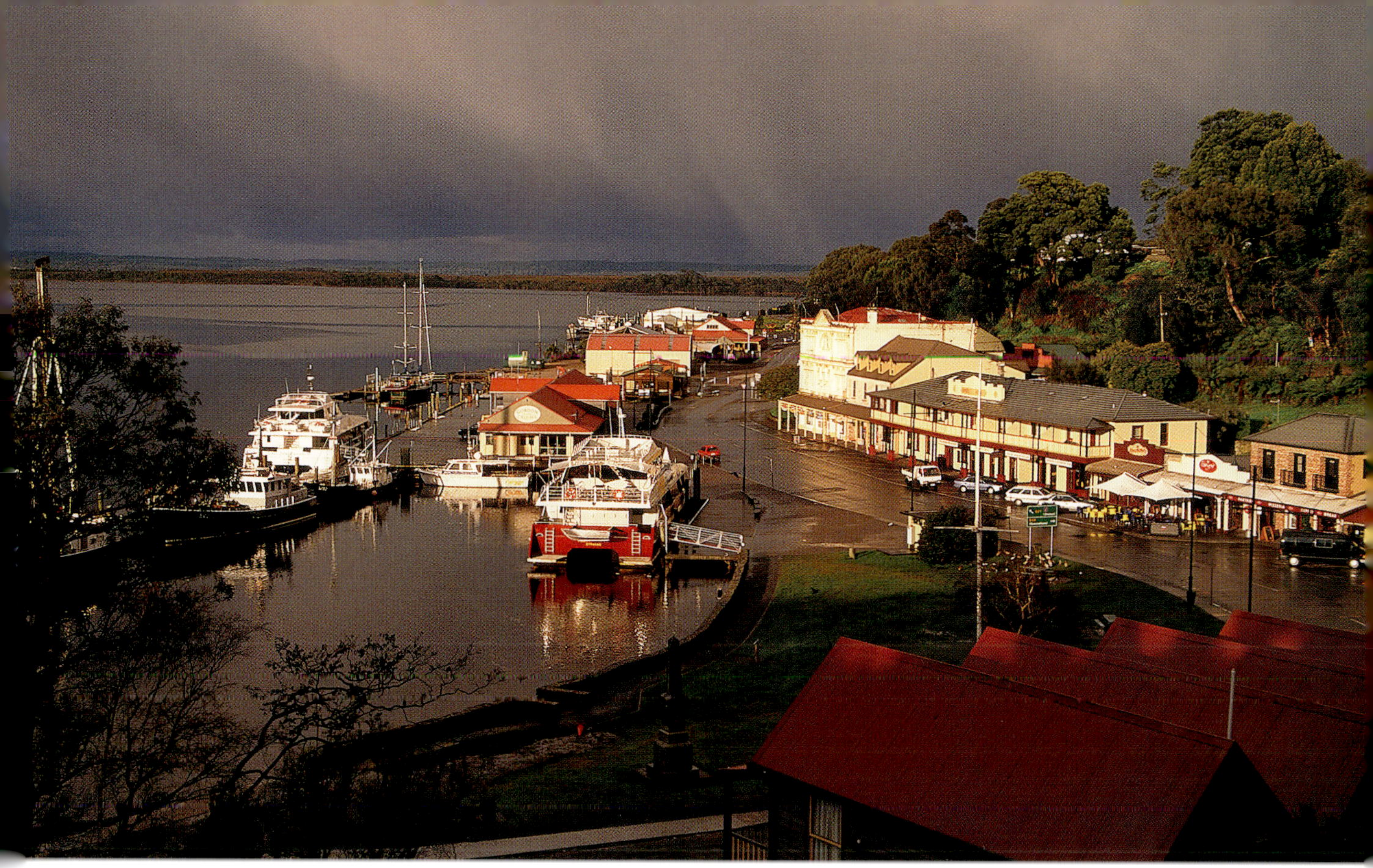

Historic Strahan, where the Gordon River wilderness cruises and scenic flights depart.

THE EAST

When travelling from Hobart the first contact with the East coast is at the seaside town of Orford. Immediately to the East of Orford and clearly dominating the horizon is Maria Island, a former penal settlement. The island is easily accessible by a short ferry trip from Triabunna.

As one travels north towards Swansea the road winds its way along the very edge of Great Oyster bay.

Schouten Island and Freycinet Peninsula create the back-drop to this beautiful area.

The East Coast like inland Tasmania was subject to early 19th century settlement with land grants to free settlers. Evidence of convict labour can be seen in several stone buildings and bridges such as Spiky Bridge, just south of Swansea.

A thriving whaling industry was also a part of the East Coast's early 19th century history.

The Swansea Bark Mill Museum and tea room is an attraction not to be missed for a display of the East Coast's indigenous and early European history.

A generally milder and dryer climate has made the East Coast popular for Tasmanians and tourists alike. Adding to this is the spectacular Freycinet National Park with its views of Wineglass Bay, its azure blue water and Coles Bay township with a backdrop of the red granite Hazards mountains.

Further north is the holiday town of Bicheno, well known for its nightly penguin tours and the Crohill art and craft gallery. Both north and south of Bicheno stretch some of the world's most beautiful beaches and coastal drives.

St. Helens, the most northerly of the East Coast centres is well known for game fishing with several charter boats available.

Inland from St. Helens are many bush walking areas including St. Columba falls and the Blue Tier Reserve. The 'Pub in the Paddock' is also a unique attraction.

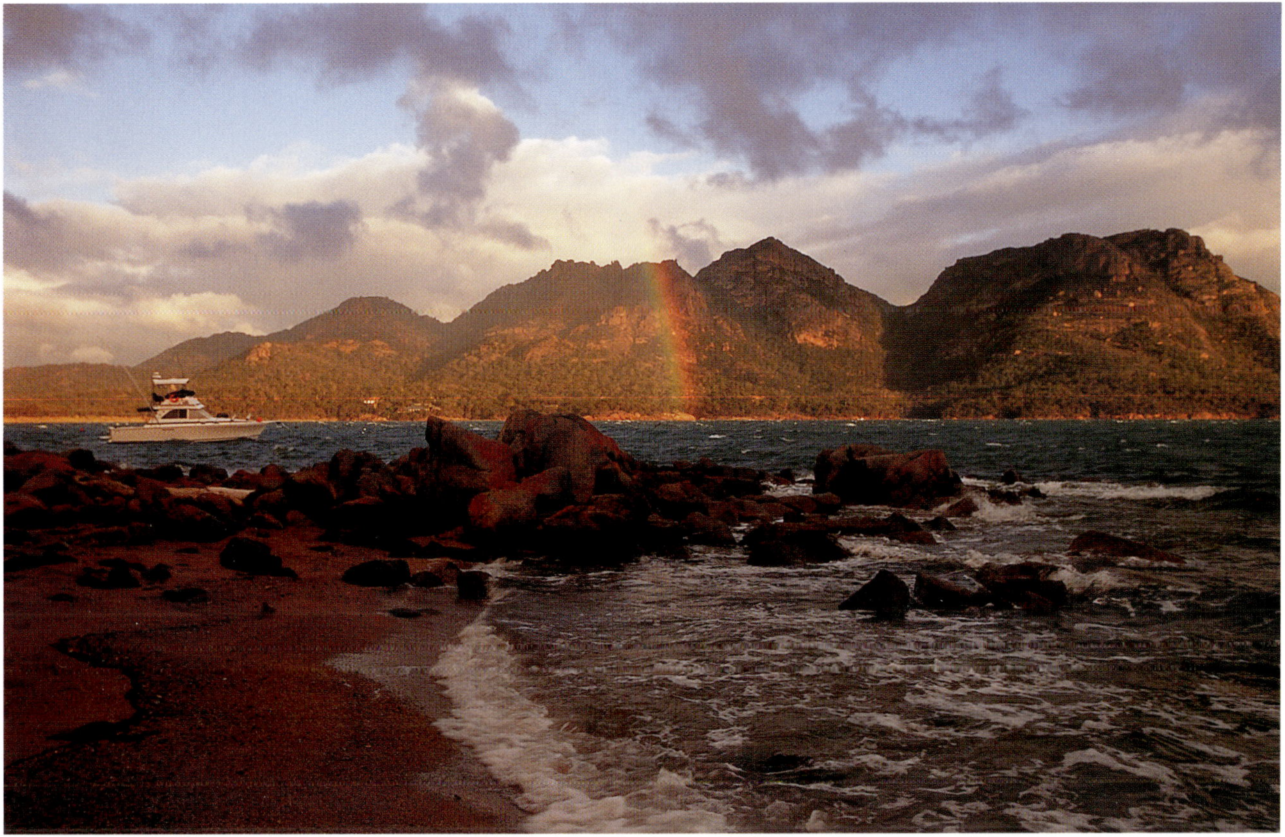

The Hazards are the backdrop to Coles Bay, Freycinet National Park.

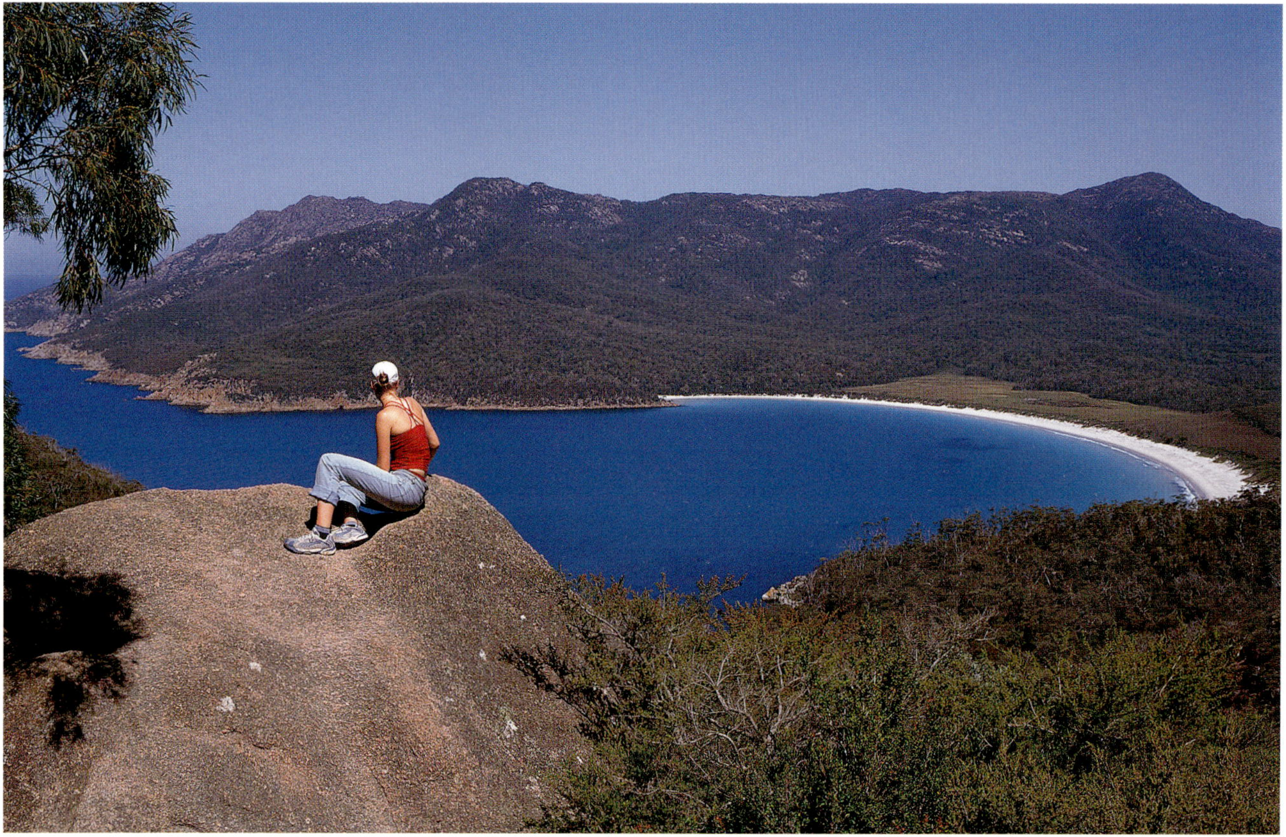

Wineglass Bay, Freycinet National Park.

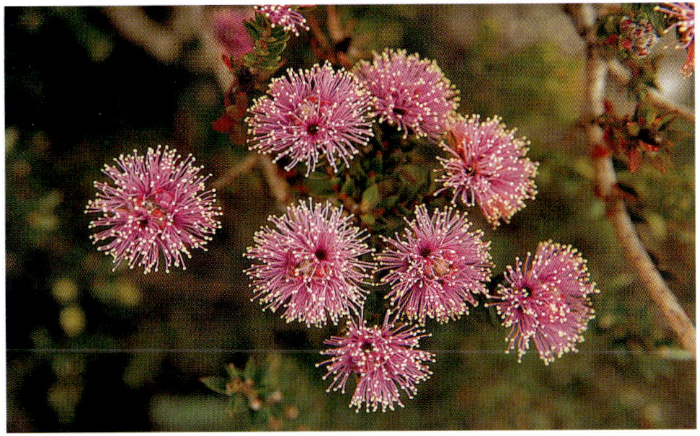

Melaleuca squamea - Swamp Melaleuca.

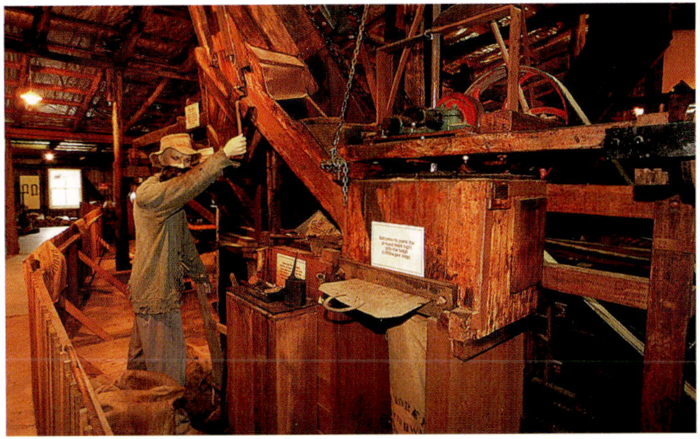

Swansea Bark Mill Museum.

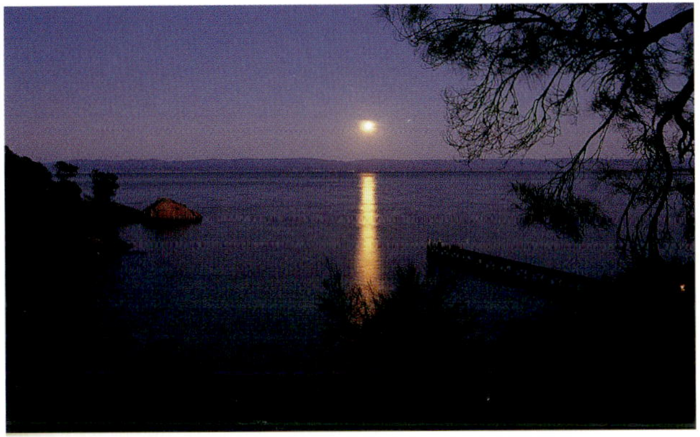

Moonlight, Freycinet Lodge Jetty.

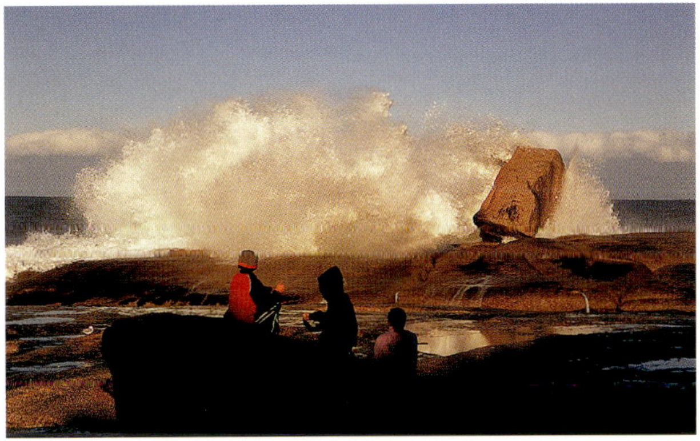

Blowhole, Bicheno.

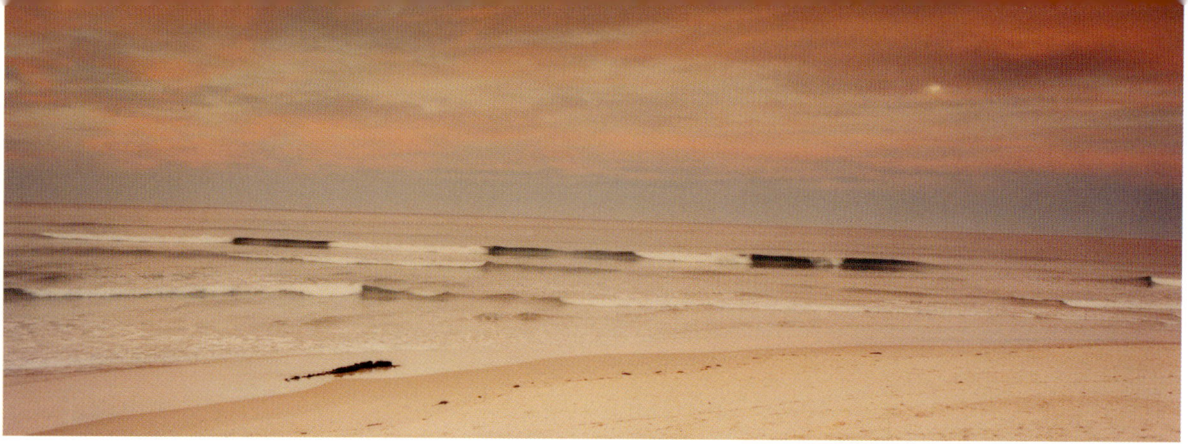

Scamander moonrise.

Summers day at Binalong Bay.

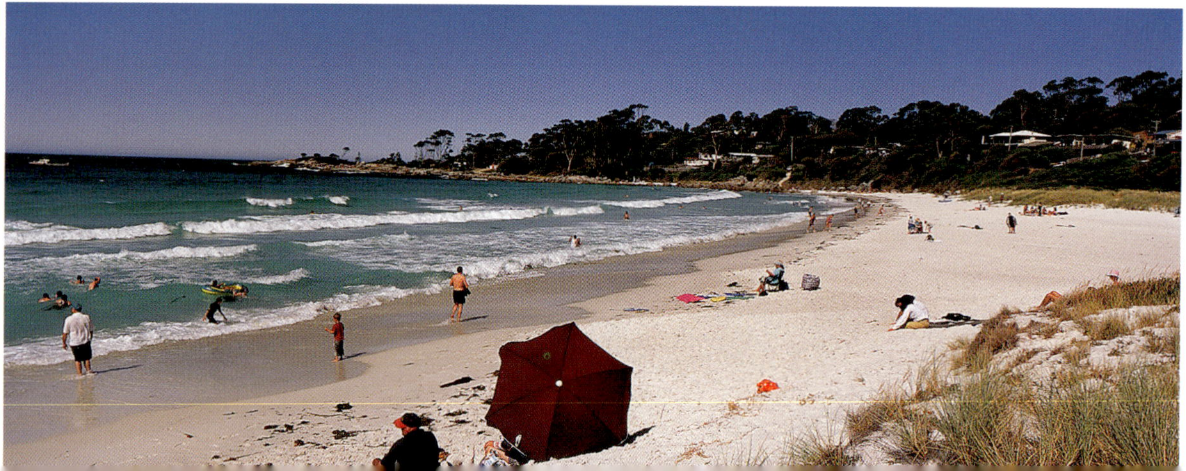

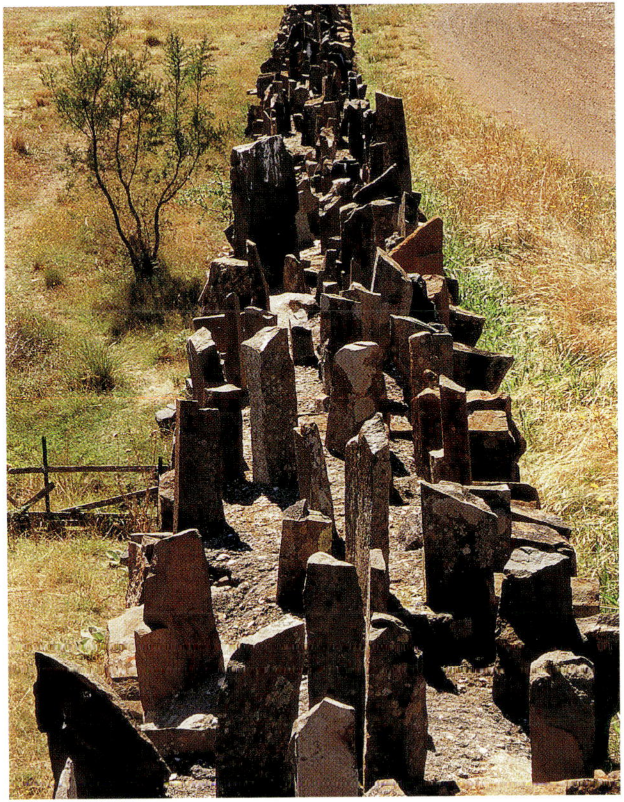

Convict built Spiky Bridge (1834) near Swansea.

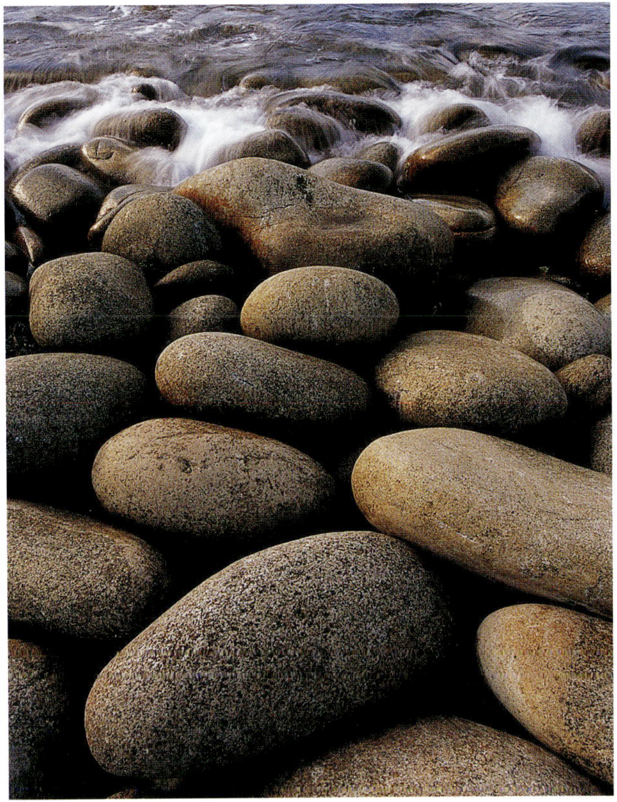

Bluestone Bay, Freycinet National Park.

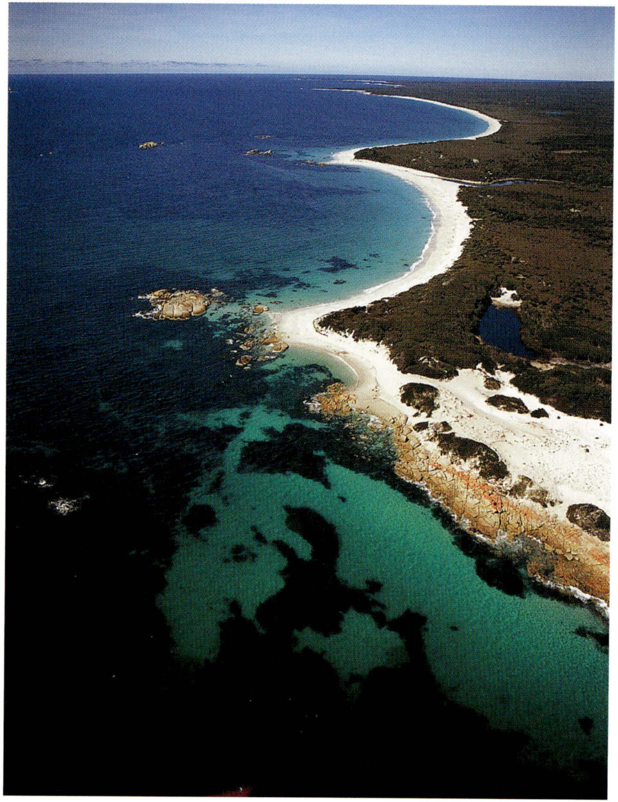

Mt. William National Park.

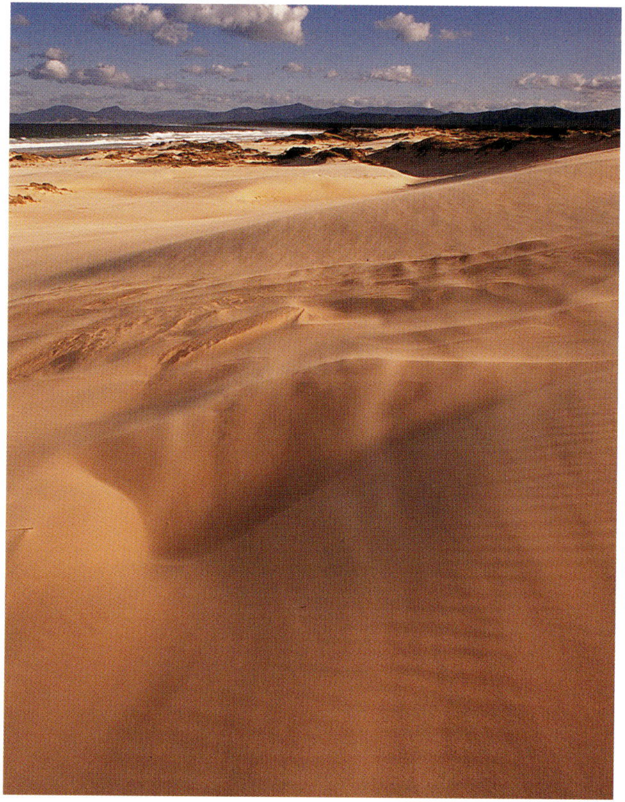

Windswept Peron Dunes, St. Helens Point.

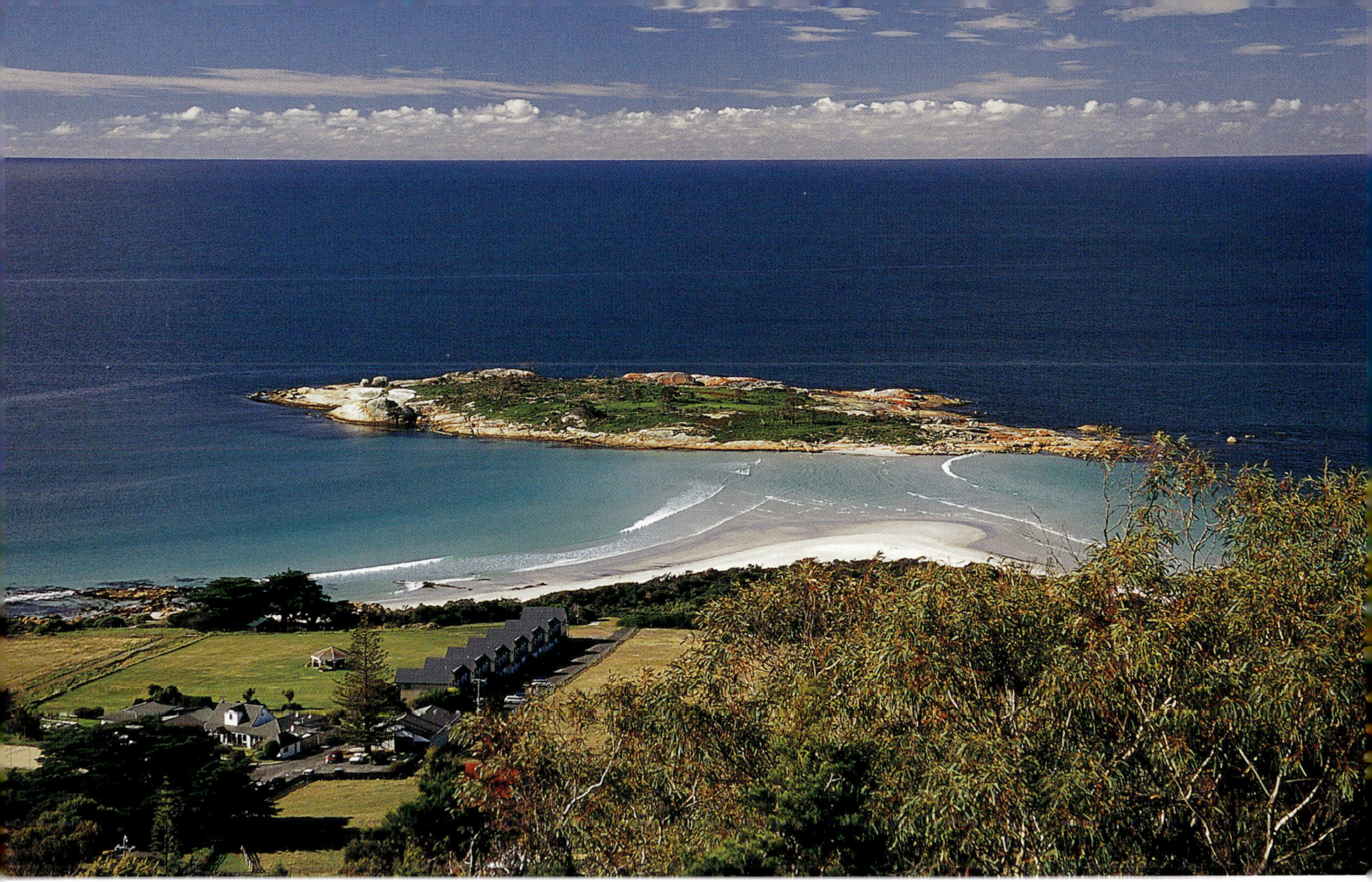

Bicheno's Diamond Island with Diamond Island Resort and Bicheno Penguin Tours viewing area on the left.

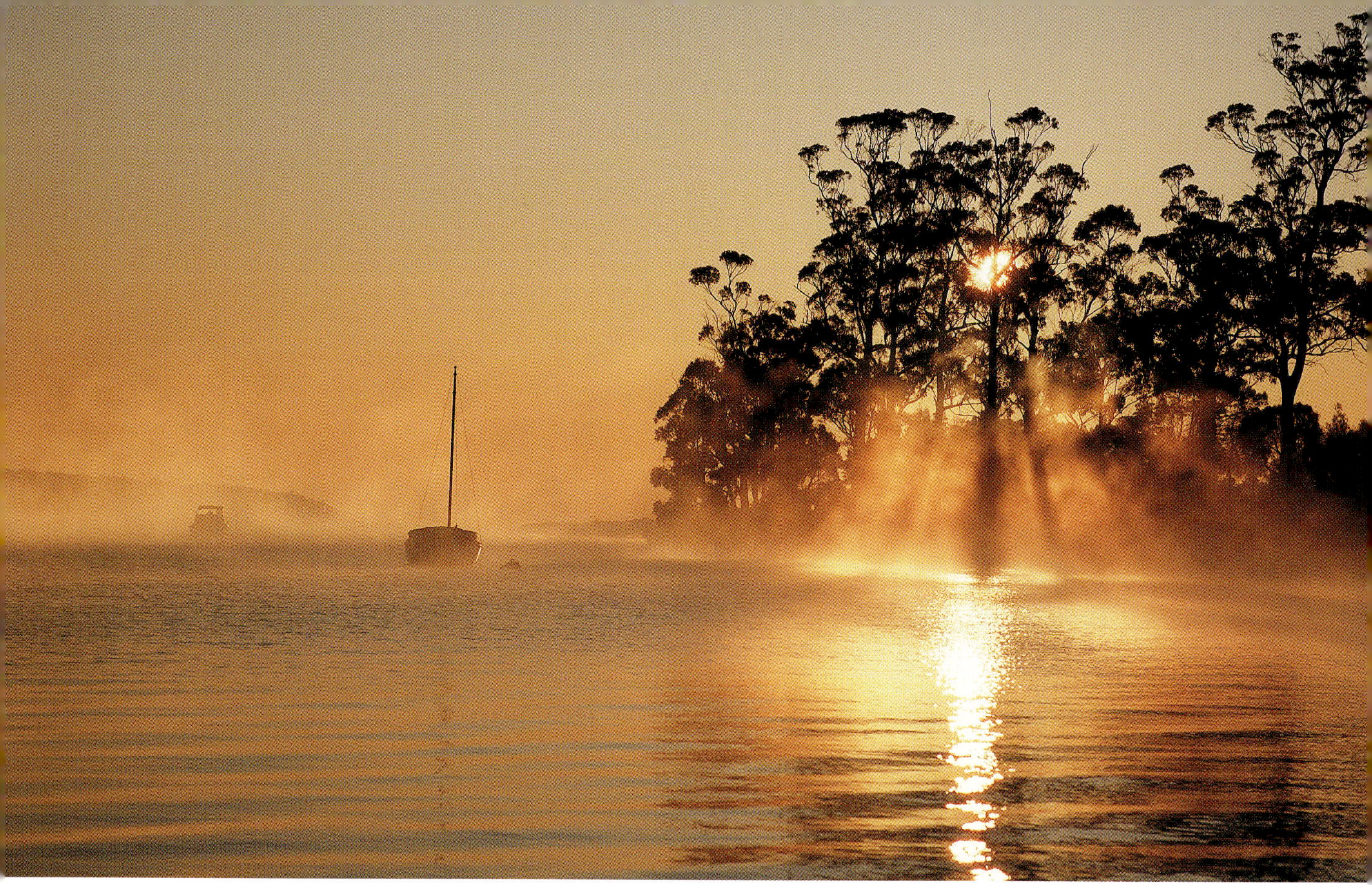

Winter dawn on Georges Bay, St. Helens.

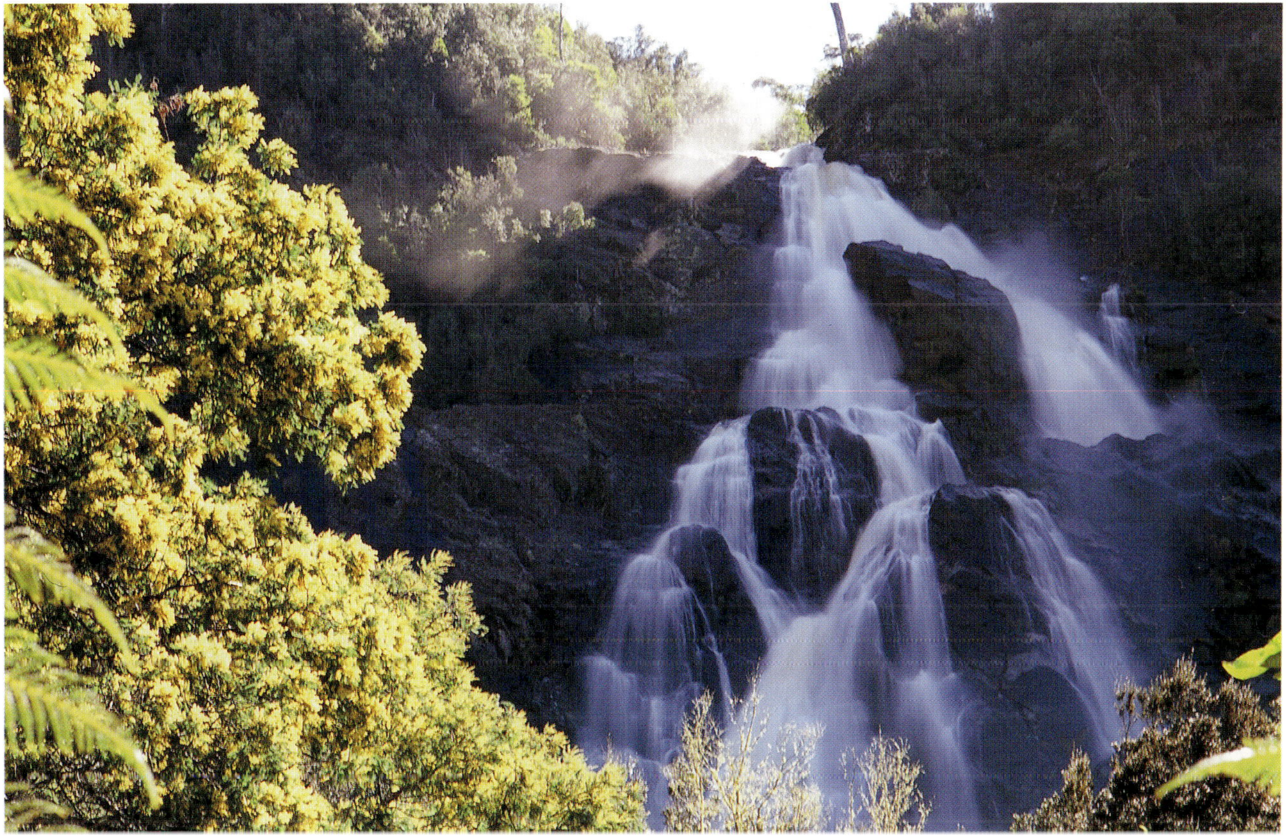

St. Columba Falls at Pyengana.

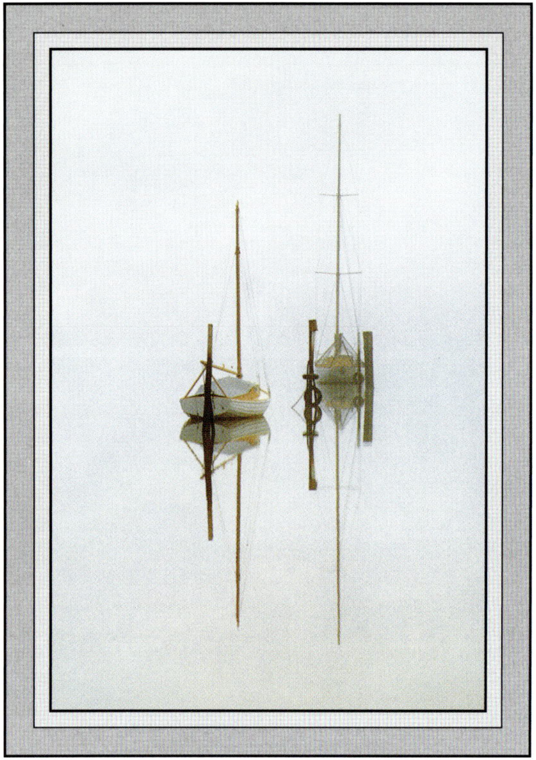

'Rivermist Suspension'
Tamar River, Tasmania

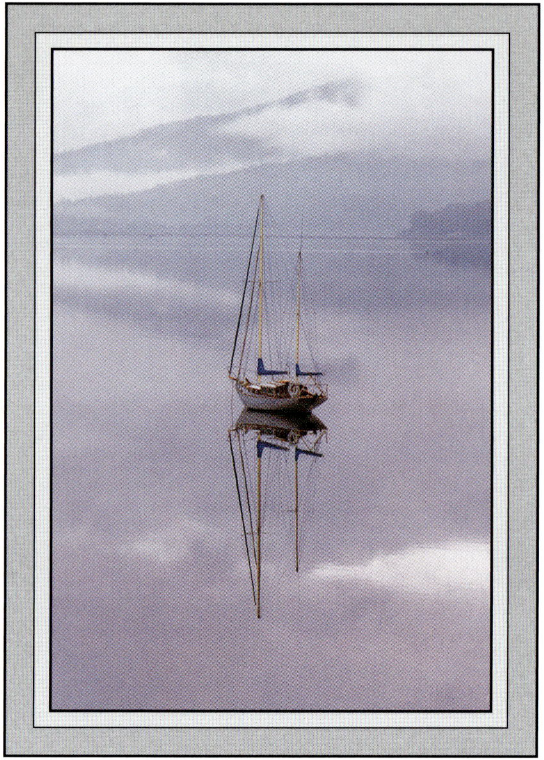

'Huon Solitaire'
Huon River, Tasmania

These two limited edition prints are available for home or office decor. They are printed in two sizes: 16 x 24 inch ($175.00 unframed) and 20 x 33 inch ($275.00 unframed). For contact details see page 1.